The Great War
'Hell's Last Horror'

NEIL DEMARCO

Contents

Chapter 1	War Breaks Out	2
Chapter 2	Why Were Some Men Unwilling to Fight?	4
Chapter 3	Propaganda and Censorship	6
Chapter 4	Nations at War	8
Chapter 5	Why Wasn't the War Over by Christmas?	10
Chapter 6	Trench Warfare: Stalemate	12
Chapter 7	Attempts to Break the Stalemate	14
Chapter 8	Life in the Trenches	16
Chapter 9	The Experience of Battle	18
Chapter 10	How Did Soldiers View Their Enemies?	22
Chapter 11	The Great War on the Western Front: Outline	24
Chapter 12	The War on Other Fronts: Gallipoli and Italy	26
Chapter 13	The Eastern Front	28
Chapter 14	New Weapons: Gas and Aircraft	30
Chapter 15	New Weapons: The Tank	32
Chapter 16	The Battle of the Somme – Lions Led by Donkeys?	34
Chapter 17	Verdun and Passchendaele	38
Chapter 18	Jutland – War Winner?	40
Chapter 19	The U-Boat Campaign and America's Entry into the War	42
Chapter 20	Why Did Germany Lose the War?	46
Chapter 21	Women and the Great War: The Home Front	48
Chapter 22	Women and the Great War: The Military Front	52
Chapter 23	The Impact of the War on the Civilian Population	54
Chapter 24	The Great War and the Cinema	60
Chapter 25	The Great War Today	62
Glossary		64
Index		Inside back cover

War Breaks Out

Why was there a war? Was it a popular idea? Why did men volunteer?

The simple answer to why war broke out in 1914 is that none of the great powers tried that hard to avoid it. Tension between the leading powers in Europe had existed for over two decades and gradually two alliance groups had come into existence.

Britain, France and Russia formed alliances or agreements with each other because they all shared a common fear. They all felt threatened by Germany. France felt threatened by Germany's large army. This fear was mixed with a desire for revenge because the Germans had seized two French provinces, Alsace and Lorraine, on the French-German border in a war in 1871.

Britain had become anxious about the growth of Germany's navy. The British feared it could be used in a war to cut Britain off from its Empire and vital supplies. Russia's worry was more to do with Germany's ally, Austria. Russia and Austria competed against each other for influence in the Balkans region of south-east Europe.

By 1914 two strong alliance systems were in place. The Entente Powers of Britain, France and Russia faced the Central Powers of Germany and Austria. In June 1914 the war was triggered off by the assassination of the heir to the throne of the Austrian Empire. The Austrian government blamed Serbia and declared war on Serbia on 28 July 1914. At this point the various alliance agreements kicked in. Germany came into the war in support of Austria, and Russia came to the assistance of Serbia. Within a week, Britain and France were also at war with the Central Powers.

Franz Ferdinand, the heir to the throne of the Austrian Empire, and his pregnant wife were assassinated together.

The war had been long expected. Governments and peoples were ready for it and, it must be said, many actually wanted it. Few realised that this war, the Great War, would turn out to be, in the words of the British poet, Siegfried Sassoon, 'Hell's Last Horror'.

Why did men volunteer?

During August and September 1914 736 000 Britons volunteered for the British army. By 1916 2.5 million had done so. Their reasons varied. Most went to fight out of a sense of patriotism, honour and duty. They believed that it was their duty to fight for their country and that it was a matter of honour. Britain and its Empire seemed to be threatened by the 'beastly Huns', as the Germans were often described in the propaganda of the time.

Not all men enlisted for honour or duty. To the unemployed even the average army pay of nine or ten shillings a week was better than nothing and encouraged some to join up. This was about a third of what an unskilled worker earned in a week but only a little less than an apprentice.

A The alliance system in Europe in 1914.

Map labels: BRITAIN, RUSSIA, Eastern Front, GERMANY, BELGIUM, Western Front, AUSTRIA-HUNGARY, FRANCE, Italian Front, ROMANIA (1916), Black Sea, ITALY (1915), SERBIA, BULGARIA (1915), TURKEY, GREECE (1917), Mediterranean Sea

0   500 km

Legend:
- Germany and her allies
- Britain and her allies
- Joined war on Britain's side (with year in brackets)
- Joined war on Germany's side (with year in brackets)

B This photograph shows a batch of volunteers with their recruiting sergeant. Look at the way the men are dressed. What can you tell about the social classes and ages of men who volunteered for the war?

Pals' battalions

The glamour of a uniform and the chance for adventure attracted a good number of young men – especially since everybody expected the war to be over by the Christmas of 1914. In the meantime, men who volunteered together were promised that they could fight together in what became known as the 'Pals' battalions'. Men from the same towns or cities formed regiments like the 'Sheffield Pals' or the 'Barnsley Pals'. Former pupils at private schools also formed their own battalions. These regiments had tremendous morale because they knew each other or came from the same area.

Peer group pressure was hard to resist. If all your workmates were joining up, it was easier to go along with the crowd. It took courage to resist this. It took even more courage when men out of uniform were handed white feathers by women as a sign of their 'cowardice'. If you weren't in uniform you could find it hard to get served in pubs. Sergeant Thomas Painting was taken prisoner in 1915 but escaped from a prison camp in Germany. He walked to the Danish frontier and from there he

made his way back to England. On arriving in England in civilian clothes he was promptly handed a white feather! History does not record his reaction. For one reason or another, it seemed a lot simpler to sign up for a war which would be 'over by Christmas', anyway.

D The historian, Denis Winter, describes the reasons some men volunteered for the army in *Death's Men* (1979):

Bert Warrant joined the 10th Londons after robbing the Hackney Empire [a cinema] of £300. Private Jenkins took similar evasive action from police in hot pursuit after he had looted German shops in Billingsgate. Men arrested after the lootings of 17 October 1914 in Deptford High Street, which were aimed at German shops, were given the choice of 18 months' hard labour or immediate join-up.

E Until 1916 the government relied on *persuading* men to fight, using recruitment posters like this one.

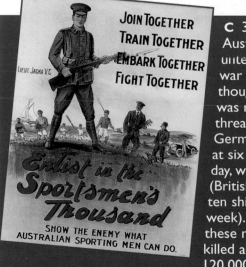

JOIN TOGETHER
TRAIN TOGETHER
EMBARK TOGETHER
FIGHT TOGETHER

LIEUT JACKA V.C.

Enlist in the Sportsmen's Thousand
SHOW THE ENEMY WHAT AUSTRALIAN SPORTING MEN CAN DO.

C 330 000 Australians volunteered for the war – even though Australia was not directly threatened by Germany. The pay, at six shillings a day, was attractive (British troops got ten shillings a week). 59 000 of these men were killed and another 120 000 wounded.

Q

1 What evidence is there that the war was popular with many men at the very start?
2 Why do you think the government was keen to set up 'Pals' battalions'?
3 Why do you think the 'white feather' campaign was so effective in persuading men to enlist?
4 What does source D suggest about the reasons why some men enlisted?
5 What reasons does source E give for men to volunteer?
6 Source D's interpretation to explain why men enlisted is different to source E. How can you explain this difference? (Think about the **provenance** of each source – when was it published? What was its purpose?)

Why Were Some Men Unwilling to Fight?

Men clearly had many different reasons for supporting the war – patriotism, duty, a sense of adventure, a chance to escape poverty or even prison. But there was also a tiny minority who opposed the war because of their personal beliefs. In January 1916 the government introduced **conscription**. This meant that most single, fit men aged between 18 and 41 now had to serve in one of the armed services. In March this was extended to married men as well. Conscription was necessary because not enough men were volunteering. In December 1915 only 55 000 volunteered, compared with 436 000 in September 1914.

The Military Service Act of January 1916 excused from service men in essential or 'reserved' occupations, such as miners and shipyard workers, and 'those who could show a conscientious objection'. Tribunals were set up to hear the cases of conscientious objectors (COs). These were men who would not fight on the grounds of conscience. 16 000 men were registered as COs.

A The popular attitude to conscientious objectors was a harsh one. This Australian poster suggests that men who avoided the war were taking the coward's way out. How else does the poster try to shame such men?

B This Australian recruitment poster was one of many which helped to persuade 330 000 Australians to volunteer for the war.

Reasons to object – Part One

COs gave a variety of different reasons. Some objected to the war because of their religious views: they were **pacifist** Christians, like Quakers, and opposed violence in all circumstances. Others were not pacifists but objected to this war in particular. These men were **socialists** and refused to kill their fellow workers, whether they were Germans or not. They believed the war was being fought to make money for the wealthy factory owners.

The vast majority of these COs agreed to do some kind of service which was helpful to the war effort but which would keep them out of combat. Some became stretcher bearers or worked on farms. A small minority, about 1500 men, refused to do even this. They were **absolutists** and refused to do anything which would help the war. They argued that agreeing to do farmwork, for example, simply allowed another man to fight and pull the trigger in their place. These absolutists were sent to do hard labour in prison. When the war ended, the authorities kept them in prison for another six months so that the returning troops would get whatever jobs were going. They were also stopped from voting in elections until 1926.

Reasons to object – Part Two

Some men were unwilling to fight for more practical reasons than those of COs. It is possible that the most enthusiastic volunteers for the war were either the very rich or the poor. The privileged upper classes of England were as patriotic as any group but they also had employees to look after their estates and concerns while they were away. The very poor had no businesses to worry about and often not even a job to leave. But the self-employed faced real problems if they enlisted. What would happen to their small businesses?

There were many self-employed men among those who appeared before tribunals to argue that they should be allowed to stay out of the army. One farmer tried to bribe a recruiting sergeant to delay his call-up so he could get the harvest in. He was fined 25 pounds – at a time when the average worker earned 90 pounds in a year. On average, about four in every five men who appeared before a tribunal had their claim accepted.

Not all those who appeared before tribunals, though, had convincing excuses. The man who said he should be excused war service because he had to bring his wife tea in bed every morning had his appeal turned down!

In 1916 Britain was fighting a desperate war against a powerful enemy. No one knew who would win but everyone knew just how many lives the war had already cost. In these circumstances, the government deserves credit for allowing the principle that some men had good reasons not to fight. Conscientious objectors were very unpopular with the public and some criticised the government for allowing 'cowards' or 'skivers' to get out of doing their duty.

> Tribunals hearing the pleas of men opposed to the war accepted 80 per cent of the cases they heard.

C Frederic Manning fought in the Great War and in 1929 published a novel, *The Middle Parts of Fortune*, in which one of the characters, Weeper Smart, is asked why he volunteered for the war:

'That's where you've got me beat, lad,' he admitted. 'When I saw all them as didn't know any better than we did joinin' up, and I went walkin' out wi' me girl on Sundays, as usual, I just felt ashamed ... until in the end it got me down ... and like a bloody fool, I went and joined up. But I tell thee now, that if I were once out of these togs and in civilian clothes again, I wouldn't mind all the shame in the world ... Let them as made the war come and fight it, that's what I say.'

Q

1 Why did some men become conscientious objectors?
2 What do the statistics quoted on volunteers for the army suggest about support for the war?
3 Do you think that men and women should have the right to refuse to help their country in a war which they oppose because of their personal beliefs?
4 What basic reason does Weeper give for joining the army?
5 Who do you think he has in mind when he says 'Let them as made the war come and fight it ... '?
6 Can you suggest why Manning's book would not have been published during the war or immediately after it? Explain your answer.

Propaganda and Censorship

Do governments have the right to lie in wartime?

Propaganda

Before the introduction of conscription in January 1916 the government relied on volunteers for its armed forces. It used various **propaganda** techniques to encourage men to enlist. Propaganda involves the use of ideas to persuade people to believe certain things or behave in a certain way. Sometimes propaganda involves the use of deliberate lies to achieve this effect. The British government during the Great War certainly made little effort to check the truth of its stories when it published reports about German 'atrocities' – as the Bryce Commission affair makes clear.

The Bryce Commission

Stories of the atrocities committed by the Germans against 'gallant little Belgium' led many to enlist. A report by Lord Bryce (May 1915) into these 'atrocities' was translated into 30 languages. The report told of the rape of 20 Belgian girls in public at Liege and of how eight soldiers had bayoneted a two-year-old child. Another German soldier had sliced off the breasts of a peasant girl. But Bryce's committee did not interview a single witness to these events. The reports were supposed to be based on 1200 statements taken from Belgian refugees in Britain but no trace of these interviews has ever been found.

A Belgian investigation in 1922 could find no evidence to support these claims either. By then, of course, the Bryce Commission report had achieved its purpose in stoking up hatred against the Germans. However, clearly some 5000 Belgian civilians did die during the German advance into Belgium. Some were shot as reprisals or simply killed as the result of the fighting.

The soap factory myth

Another successful piece of British propaganda concerned the atrocity story about German soap factories.

In April 1917 *The Times* ran a story about the Germans melting down human corpses to extract glycerine for soap. The author of this nonsense was probably the British chief of military intelligence. He had two photographs in his file. One showed corpses awaiting burial and the other dead horses on their way to a soap factory. He simply swapped the captions around and passed the photographs on to *The Times*.

However, the British government did pay a price for using propaganda like this. 30 years later in the Second World War there were stories of even more terrible crimes

RED CROSS OR IRON CROSS?

WOUNDED AND A PRISONER OUR SOLDIER CRIES FOR WATER.

THE GERMAN "SISTER" POURS IT ON THE GROUND BEFORE HIS EYES.

THERE IS NO WOMAN IN BRITAIN WHO WOULD DO IT.

THERE IS NO WOMAN IN BRITAIN WHO WILL FORGET IT.

A German 'atrocities' played a major part in British propaganda. Posters such as this one were designed to make the public feel outraged and determined to get revenge.

During the first year of the war 2.5 million copies of 110 different Government propaganda posters were issued.

To prevent this —

BUY
WAR SAVINGS
CERTIFICATES
NOW

B A poster to persuade people to invest in the war effort by warning of what Britain would be like if Germany won.

The military authorities claimed that such news was bad for public morale and that it should be censored. Others argued that censorship was more about protecting the image and reputation of the army leaders than the national interest.

The Church

The Church of England was keen to give its support to the war effort. Sometimes this support was a little over the top. One clergyman claimed that the Germans planned to kill every British male child if they won the war. Some bishops, though, in 1917 reminded Christians that it was their duty to love their enemies – even Germans. They were attacked for undermining morale.

committed by the Germans against civilian populations – including stories about corpses used for soap. The British public was reluctant to believe this 'propaganda'. This time, though, the crimes were real.

Censorship

Preventing the population from learning of bad news is another way of controlling and shaping people's attitudes. Newspaper and radio reports were heavily **censored** to keep details of defeats from the public. News of the disaster at Gallipoli (see Chapter 12) was censored and would have stayed that way until after the war, if it hadn't been for the actions of an Australian journalist called Keith Murdoch. Murdoch was arrested and his story confiscated but it still got out. The news led to the dismissal of the commander of the Gallipoli forces.

Q

1 What feelings are sources A and B trying to arouse in the public? Make specific references to each poster.
2 Which of the two posters has the greater appeal to patriotism?
3 Which of the two posters do you think would have been the more effective in encouraging anti-German feelings? Give reasons for your answer.
4 What effect do you think the Bryce Commission report had on public opinion in Britain? Explain your answer.
5 Was the government right to make use of the Bryce Commission report in its propaganda against the Germans – even if it knew the report was inaccurate?
6 Is it right for the army to keep from the public reports about defeats in wars?
7 An American senator said in 1917 that 'The first casualty when war comes is the truth.' What do you suppose he meant by this and was he right?

Nations at War

What wins wars?

This chapter looks at some of the factors that are important in deciding the outcome of a war. Clearly weapons of war, such as shells, artillery, rifles and ships are vital. To make these, countries need large supplies of coal, iron and steel. But weapons and **raw materials** are of no use if the soldiers at the front are not willing to fight or if the population at home is against the war.

The politicians and the people of Europe all expected a short war. 'Over by Christmas' was heard time and time again. But the war lasted four years rather than four months. So why were the Allies so confident that it would be a short war?

Morale

Good morale is important for winning wars. Those fighting the war needed to believe in their country's cause. Was there any evidence in 1914 that any of the major countries at war suffered from poor morale? Soldiers who were not committed would not fight well. The morale of the civilians at home was just as important as the morale at the front. Was there any evidence that the men and women at home did not support the troops in the front line?

> One machine-gun had the fire-power of 60 riflemen.

A A German soldier, Carl von Clemm, tells of his feelings when war broke out (from *People's Century* by G Hodgson, 1995).

It is normal all over the world with young fellows who see war as just an adventure, and it is patriotism and it is partly to get decorations ... We believed God was on our side ... we felt we were defending ourselves and I was very anxious to be a normal patriot and help defend my country.

B French civilians and new recruits at the beginning of the war.

C German civilians giving their troops an enthusiastic send-off in 1914.

Military might

Allied Powers	Soldiers	Battleships
Britain	710 000 (volunteers)	64
France	1 250 000	28
Russia	1 200 000	16
Central Powers		
Germany	2 200 000	40
Austria-Hungary	810 000	16

D Military strength in 1914.

Allied Powers	Coal (in tons)	Iron (in tons)	Steel (in tons)
Britain	292 000 000	11 000 000	6 500 000
France	40 000 000	5 000 000	3 500 000
Russia	36 000 000	4 000 000	4 000 000
Central Powers			
Germany	277 000 000	15 000 000	14 000 000
Austria-Hungary	47 000 000	2 000 000	3 000 000

E Industrial strength in 1914: production in millions of tons. Italy has been left out because its raw material output in 1914 was very low (less than a million tons of coal, for example).

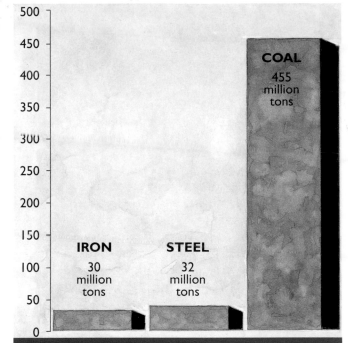

F The industrial strength of the United States in 1914: production in millions of tons. The USA joined the Allies Britain, France and Russia in April 1917.

Q

1 What do sources A, B and C suggest about the morale of troops and civilians on both sides at the start of the war?
2 a) Look at source D. Add up the total number of (i) soldiers and (ii) battleships for the Allies. Now do the same for the Central Powers.
   b) Which side was the most powerful in military terms?
   c) Does your answer help explain why the Allies were so sure that it would be a short war?
3 a) Add up the outputs for each side for (i) coal, (ii) iron, and (iii) steel. Do not include the USA.
   b) Which side was the most powerful in industrial terms?
4 What impact do you think the entry of the United States had on which side would win the war?
5 What does this exercise tell you about the dangers of making judgements based on only some of the statistical evidence available (by using source E and not source F)?
6 'The British were right to expect a quick victory over the Germans in 1914.' Using the sources, and your own knowledge, explain whether you agree or not with this interpretation.

Why Wasn't the War Over by Christmas?

If the German Schlieffen Plan had worked, the war might have been over in 1914 – and won by Germany. This chapter sets out to explain what the plan was and why it failed.

The German war plan was finalised by General Schlieffen in 1905. Schlieffen was certain that Germany would soon have to fight a war on two fronts: a war against the Russians in the east and a war against the French in the west. He knew that Germany could not win a two-front war. His plan was to knock France out of the war in just six weeks. After this, the Germans could deal with the Russians on their own.

The Plan in detail

Schlieffen knew that the French would be desperate to get back the two provinces of Alsace and Lorraine that they had lost to the Germans in the war of 1870–71. He deliberately kept the German forces guarding these eastern provinces weak. He hoped this would encourage the French to attack there, leaving the way clear for a surprise German attack from the north.

Schlieffen planned that the troops not used in Alsace-Lorraine would support the main attack in the north. 90 per cent of Germany's forces in the west would invade France through Belgium and Holland. Paris would be captured and then the French would surrender. Once Germany had beaten the French, it could send its troops to the east to deal with the Russians.

The success of the Plan depended on three things. Firstly, the army in the north had to be very large and it would need troops from the southern army guarding Alsace-Lorraine. Secondly, the soldiers in the northern army would have to cover 35 kilometres a day. To do this, they would need excellent logistics. Logistics is the ability to keep troops in battle supplied with food, ammunition, and other needs. Thirdly, it was assumed that the Russians would take at least three months to get their army ready to fight.

Schlieffen died in 1913 and General von Moltke, the new Chief of Staff, took over his plan. But von Moltke lacked the nerve to take all the troops he needed from the army in Alsace-Lorraine. Instead of using 90 per cent of his troops in the northern army, he only used 60 per cent – about one million men. He was afraid the southern army would not be able to hold back a determined French attack on Alsace-Lorraine unless it had more men. To make matters worse, Moltke decided to send 100 000 troops over to the Eastern Front because the Russians had **mobilised** their army in just six weeks and not the expected 12.

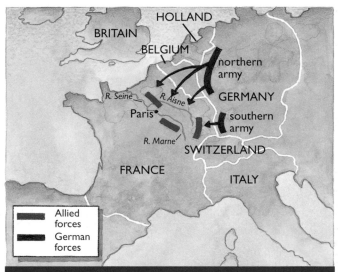

A The Schlieffen Plan in action. The German northern army swept down through Belgium into France. The southern army moved a short distance into eastern France.

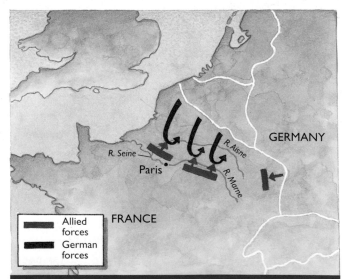

B The Allied counter-attack. The French and British forces stopped the Germans south of the River Marne and then drove them back. The Germans retreated to the River Aisne and there both sides dug in.

The outcome

Moltke gave the order to attack France and Belgium on 4 August. The Schlieffen Plan had begun. Even with their smaller numbers, the northern armies made rapid progress as they swept back the Belgian, French and small British forces in their way. But the Germans were advancing too quickly. Their supplies could not keep up and the troops became exhausted. Then, when the Germans were just 60 kilometres from Paris, the French and British counter-attacked along the River Marne.

The Battle of the Marne (5–10 September) was the most important battle of the war. It saved Paris from capture and therefore wrecked the Schlieffen Plan. The defeat of the Plan meant Germany would have to fight the French and Russians at the same time. Germany could not win such a war. Schlieffen had known that and so did Moltke. Moltke told the German Kaiser (Emperor): 'Your Majesty, we have lost the war'. Kaiser William promptly sacked him.

Stalemate

The Allies drove the Germans back from the Marne to another river, the Aisne. Here both sides dug in and the pattern for the war was set. It would be a war fought from trenches. Gradually, both sides dug a series of trenches which stretched from the Belgian coast to the Swiss border – 700 kilometres. The Western Front moved only a little during the next four years. The land around it came to resemble a long, muddy brown scar across the face of France and Belgium.

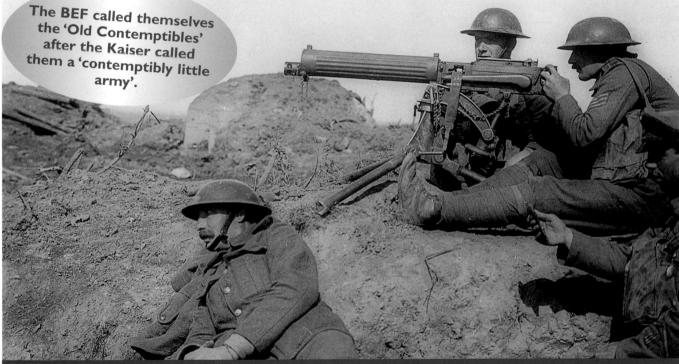

The BEF called themselves the 'Old Contemptibles' after the Kaiser called them a 'contemptibly little army'.

C The machine-gun, along with trenches and barbed wire, gave the defenders the edge over attackers. This British Vickers machine-gun could fire around 500 bullets a minute. Weapons like this made sure that any attack would be very costly for the attacking side.

---

1 What kind of war did General Schlieffen hope to avoid with his Plan?
2 On what three factors did the Schlieffen Plan depend for its success?
3 Why did Moltke reduce the size of the northern armies? Why was this change so important?
4 Do you think Moltke's decision to send 100 000 troops to the Eastern Front had an important effect on the Schlieffen Plan's chances of success? Explain your answer.
5 You have been asked by the Kaiser to write a 25-line report (the Kaiser doesn't like reading much) on Moltke's handling of the Schlieffen Plan. Point out any good or bad points in his performance and recommend what action the Kaiser should take.

Trench Warfare: *Stalemate*

Why was it so difficult to break through the enemy's trenches?

Both sides dug trenches during the winter of 1914–15 and waited for the weather to improve before launching new attacks in the spring. But the war never became the war both sides had expected. Cavalry played no useful part and infantry attacks offered only target practice for the defenders.

Trenches were very difficult to capture since a trench system consisted of at least three lines of trenches. The front-line trench was backed up by the support trench and behind that was the reserve trench. These trenches were connected to each other by communication trenches. Each trench was protected by rows of barbed wire up to 30 metres deep. Each section of trench would have a fire-step from which a soldier could fire or – briefly – observe the enemy trenches. Trenches were usually zigzagged so that if the enemy captured one they would not be able to fire down its length. This shape also restricted the impact of explosions in the trenches themselves.

The men also dug trenches into **No Man's Land** (the land in between enemy positions) to listen out for mining parties or enemy patrols at night. These trenches were called saps. All trenches were supposed to be deep enough to hide soldiers from enemy fire.

B This German trench shows that the Germans were not short of that vital trench weapon: the machine-gun. Here two machine-guns are no more than six or seven metres apart.

C A British intelligence report on the condition of the German trenches just before the Battle of the Somme, after a week-long British artillery bombardment.

The dug-outs are still good. The [German] men appear to remain in these dug-outs all the time and are completely sheltered.

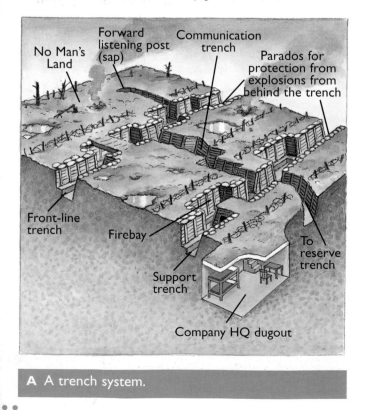

No Man's Land

Forward listening post (sap)

Communication trench

Parados for protection from explosions from behind the trench

Front-line trench

Firebay

Support trench

To reserve trench

Company HQ dugout

A A trench system.

At regular intervals there would be a machine-gun position with each machine-gun capable of firing 450–600 rounds or bullets a minute. Such fire-power proved devastating against exposed, slow-moving infantry attacking across a No Man's Land which stretched on average for 250 metres. In some cases, though, the enemy lines could be as close as 100 metres.

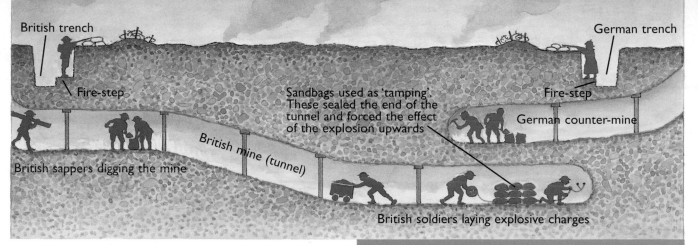

British trench

German trench

Fire-step

Sandbags used as 'tamping'. These sealed the end of the tunnel and forced the effect of the explosion upwards

Fire-step

German counter-mine

British sappers digging the mine

British mine (tunnel)

British soldiers laying explosive charges

During enemy artillery bombardments the troops could take cover in underground bunkers. The German ones were especially deep (15 metres below ground sometimes) and well constructed because they were prepared to fight a defensive war on enemy soil. They intended to stay where they were. The British and the French, though, could not afford to fight a defensive war. They had to attack to drive the Germans out of France and Belgium.

Mining operations

One of the purposes of saps (trenches dug out into No Man's Land) was to place listening posts in them. The men in these had sensitive listening equipment to pick up the sound of tunnels being dug beneath them. Both sides used mines in the war. These were explosives packed at the end of a long underground tunnel. The explosives were placed directly underneath the enemy's trench and then the tunnel was sealed. This sent the force of the explosion upwards. Mines could be very effective – if it was possible to dig them without being discovered.

E This illustration shows a mining operation. A mine has been packed into a tunnel under the German lines but a German counter-mining party is on its way. What sort of civilian job do you think gave the best preparation for this role?

When the mine was detonated, a huge explosion destroyed the enemy trench above it. At the same time the troops attacked while the enemy was in total confusion. At the start of the Third Battle of Ypres (or Passchendaele) in 1917, the British exploded 19 such mines under the German lines at the same time. Two were disconnected before the battle and their locations were lost. One went off in 1955 in an open field during a rain storm – the other is still out there.

If the enemy discovered the existence of a tunnel beneath them they would send out a counter-mining party. This would dig its way down to the tunnel to prevent the explosives being put in place. Ferocious fights, dozens of metres below ground, would often be the result.

The effects of a mining operation were often spectacular. But mines were not successful enough to allow an offensive to break through on a *wide* front.

D These British miners have reached the end of their tunnel. The officer on the left is using a pair of geophones – a device to listen out for enemy movements underground.

Q

1 What do you think the author means by 'infantry attacks offered only target practice for the defenders'?
2 Can you suggest why communication trenches (source A) were so important?
3 Why do you think it was better to dig saps into No Man's Land to listen for mining activities rather than listen from the existing trenches?
4 How do sources B and C support the idea that the Germans had strong defensive positions?
5 Using the sources, and your own knowledge, explain why it was so difficult for either side to break through the enemy lines.

Attempts to Break the Stalemate

Why did so many attacks fail?

The High Commands of both sides were keen to break through their enemy's lines. They tried very hard to do this with a series of big attacks or offensives. Only in the last year of the war did one side achieve a decisive breakthrough.

Preparations for battle

Before big attacks or offensives took place, a number of preparations were made. Large numbers of extra troops had to be brought up to the front line. Extra ammunition and supplies were needed – not to mention coffins stacked along the roadside, in full view of the advancing troops. All of these preparations would be seen by the enemy. Aerial **reconnaissance** by aircraft meant that nothing could go on behind the lines without the enemy finding out about it. However, the biggest clue to the enemy came with the heavy artillery bombardment that took place before any attack.

Artillery bombardments

Before a big offensive both sides used their artillery to shell the enemy trenches in an effort to kill troops and destroy their trenches and barbed wire defences. Before the British Somme offensive in 1916 the British bombardment, or barrage, lasted a week and over 1.5 million shells were fired along a 30 kilometre-wide front. The barrage was mostly ineffective but the Germans had no doubts as to what was going to happen next.

Most barrages stopped when the attackers were about to leave their trenches. This was to avoid shells dropping on your own men as they advanced across No Man's Land. However, sometimes planners used what was called a 'creeping 'or 'rolling' barrage. Here the barrage continued, just ahead of your own men, as the attack advanced. In this way, the enemy were kept in their dug-outs and couldn't fire at the attackers. The problem was that occasionally the shells dropped short and killed your own men.

In 1915, 1000 French artillery guns were destroyed by their own faulty shells exploding in the barrels.

A An artillery observation officer is shown here standing on the fire-step. He could be checking to see whether the shells are hitting the target. The man next to him is ready to telephone any necessary changes to the gunners.

'Over the top'

Before an attack could take place, paths had to be cut in your *own* barbed wire so your own troops could get through. This would be done at night and the paths marked with tape. This not only provided further proof of an attack but enemy machine-gunners now could direct their fire to the points where the troops would emerge.

When the order to attack was given, soldiers went 'over the top' and advanced across No Man's Land towards the enemy lines. The soldiers' task along the Somme wasn't made any easier by the order to *walk* towards the enemy. They didn't have to run, the High Command told them, because all the Germans would be killed in the barrage!

The strategy of the generals

The generals were convinced that a breakthrough would come if enough troops were concentrated along a small section of the front. In this way they would outnumber the enemy, break through, and then encircle them. After that, there would only be open countryside. But this overlooked the fact

B The New Zealand soldier in the centre is checking on enemy movements through the use of a trench periscope. The man on the left is using a 'sniperscope'. This was a rifle attached to a periscope. This allowed him to fire at any careless Germans who showed themselves above the trench line without risking his own life.

that the enemy could quickly bring in reserves from another sector to plug any gaps in their front line. This was especially easy since only a small sector of the front was under attack.

It is easy to understand why so many soldiers became bitter about their generals and the strategies they used in the war.

C The views of Private Haig (from *The First Day of the Somme* by M Middlebrook, 1971).

I cursed, and still do, the generals who caused us to suffer such torture, living in filth, eating filth, and then, death or injury, just to boost their ego.

Many historians have criticised General Haig, the commander of the British army from December 1915 until 1918, for repeatedly using tactics which cost the lives of so many. His defenders claim that, once Haig had enough tanks and artillery, these tactics finally worked in 1918 and won the war.

D Adapted from *The Price of Pity* by M Stephen (1996). General Rawlinson was in charge of the British troops at the successful Battle of Neuve Chapelle in March 1915.

Rawlinson applied intelligence and professional skill to the problem of breaking through enemy trenches. He won a victory which was effective and limited losses among his men. It was also a victory which showed Rawlinson learning on his feet, adapting to conditions which no general had ever before had to face.

E The historian, John Laffin, said this in a television programme (*Timewatch*) about General Haig:

A great commander knows exactly what he's sending his men into but Haig didn't … The principle which guided him was that if he could kill more Germans than the Germans could kill his men, then he would inevitably win. Now that is an appaling kind of strategy. It's not a strategy at all, it's just slaughter.

Q

1 Describe three ways in which the enemy could learn that an attack was being planned.
2 Which of the usual preparations do you think could have been left out to try to keep the attack a secret? Explain your answer.
3 Why was their own barbed wire a problem for attackers?
4 In what ways do sources C and D have different opinions about the generals of the war?
5 What reasons can you give to explain these different interpretations? (Think about the provenance of these sources. What differences are there between the authors of each source? Are they describing the same general or the same incident?)

Extended writing
Answer the following question in an essay of 250–300 words:

'There were no breakthroughs on the Western Front until 1918 because the generals used the wrong tactics.' What is your view of this claim? You could include in your answer the following points:

a) problems involved in launching surprise attacks;
b) the strength of the defenders' position;
c) the industrial strength of each side.

Life in the Trenches

Life in a First World War trench was mostly one of boredom and routine duties. These included replacing barbed wire, repairing and baling out flooded trenches, and digging and emptying latrines (toilets). Such duties are called 'fatigues'.

In a typical 32-day period a soldier could spend eight days in a front-line trench. Then there might be a further eight days in a reserve trench in case of an enemy attack, followed by 16 days away from the front altogether in a town or village. Every now and again, though, all this would change when an offensive took place – launched either by your side or the enemy. Then the period in the trenches could last up to six weeks before relief came through. Living conditions became extremely unpleasant, as well as dangerous.

'Trench foot'

In ideal circumstances a trench would be about two and a half metres deep with wooden duckboards along the bottom to keep feet out of the mud and water which collected there. When feet are left in water for long periods of time they can swell inside the boot, cut off circulation and rot. Frostbite could also cut off circulation. Toes were often lost in this way and sometimes even feet. This was known as 'trench foot'.

Strict measures were taken to avoid this. Men had to rub a waterproofing substance, whale oil, into their feet and soldiers would be punished if they didn't. This was necessary because some men tried to get trench foot – even at the cost of losing toes or a foot – as a way of getting a 'blighty one'.

'Blighty' was the military slang for Britain and so a blighty one was a wound serious enough to get you sent home for treatment.

> By May 1915 the British Army needed six million sandbags a month for its trenches.

Hygiene

One aspect of trench life which soldiers on both sides hated was the lack of hygiene. Latrines were pits dug in saps leading off the main trenches. They were about one and a half metres deep and were used as toilets. A plank of wood over the hole in the ground was the best on offer. When it was nearly full of waste it was supposed to be filled in and a new one dug. Soldiers weren't too keen on using these official facilities. This wasn't so much because of their revolting smell but because the enemy would occasionally lob shells into them on the off chance that someone might be in there.

BE IN THE FASHION.

Why have Cats, Dogs, Canaries, Rabbits, Parrots, etc.?

LICE !

EVERY CONCEIVABLE SHADE SUPPLIED :—BLUE BACKS, BLACK BACKS, RED BACKS, GREY BACKS, WHITE BACKS. ¶ ALSO IN A DELICATE PINK SHADE AND WITH VARIEGATED STRIPES. ¶ PURE THOROUGH-BREDS FROM OUR OWN SEAMS. ¶ MOST CLINGING, AFFECTIONATE, AND TAKING WAYS. ¶ VERY PROLIFIC, HARDY, AND WILL LIVE ANYWHERE. ¶ ONCE YOU HAVE THEM YOU WILL NEVER BE WITHOUT.

In Dainty Pochettes at 2/- per Thousand.

Write at once to E. R. M. CRACK,
Telegraphic Address : "Hitchy Koo." CHAT VILLA, CRUMBY.

B Soldiers' newsletters sometimes tried to see the funny side of louse (or chatt) infestation.

The lack of hygiene also led to lice. These are insects which feed off the blood of their hosts. Their bites cause intense itching which leads to blisters, boils and trench fever. First World War lice – or more accurately their eggs – were almost indestructible. Body heat made them hatch out of the seams of the clothes where they were often laid.

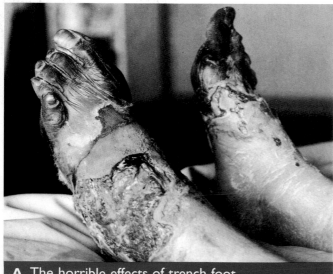

A The horrible effects of trench foot.

E Trenches – especially Allied ones – were not always built according to the manual. This one, from 1917, shows Australians in a front-line trench, during the Third Battle of Ypres.

C One Canadian wrote in his diary in 1916:

Then there is the trench cat, a strict neutral, we call him 'Wilson' [the President of the neutral USA at the time] because we found him asleep on a haversack with a rat rifling [stealing] the contents! ... He walks across No Man's Land at will and knows the meal times on both sides.

Soldiers took comfort where they could from the war's less grim aspects. The humour of the troops helped to keep them sane. Army food was a particular target for jokes. Sausages were known as 'barkers' because of the supposedly high dog-meat content in them. Cheese was called 'bung' because of the constipation it caused.

Barbed-wire defences

Sandbags

Bridge to allow support troops to cross trench

Fire-step

Duckboards

D The trenches of the Great War were supposed to look like this. Sandbags protected the soldiers at the front and the rear of the trench. In front of the sandbags was barbed wire, metres deep. A fire-step allowed the troops to raise themselves high enough to fire at the enemy when necessary.

F This photograph shows a British soldier on sentry duty while three of his exhausted comrades sleep. The picture is a puzzling one since it shows a fire-step on the left while the soldier seems to expect the enemy from the right. It is likely that this, therefore, is a captured German trench.

Q

1 Which trench in sources E and F most looks like the trench in source D? Give reasons for your answer.
2 Why do you think the trench in source E is so different from the one in source D?

3 a) What steps were taken to maintain hygiene in the trenches?
   b) Why do you think this was important?

The Experience of Battle

What was it like to fight in a battle in the First World War?

Most soldiers did not look forward to battle but accepted it. Their sense of duty played a part in giving them the courage to 'go over the top'. But what really motivated men to face death was a sense of loyalty to their fellow soldiers: comradeship. The basic desire not to let their pals down through shirking or cowardice was very powerful.

> **A** One survivor's memory (quoted in *The Price of Pity* by M Stephen, 1996).
>
> Some people say that you come to accept death, but I don't think any of us really did. It affects you terribly when a man dies, but we had some happy times because there was such a sense of comradeship, which is impossible to understand unless you have been part of it. We would all have done anything and everything to help another man.

'Copping a blighty'

If there was an honourable way out of the fighting, then soldiers would gladly take it. Being lightly wounded in the course of duty – 'copping a blighty' – was recognised by everyone as a decent way out of the fighting. However, self-inflicted wounds, such as shooting yourself in the foot, were seen as a coward's way out. 18-year-old Lance-Corporal Hiscock accidentally shot himself in the arm while cleaning some mud from his rifle. He was terrified of what might happen to him since such wounds usually meant a court-martial – an army trial. Hiscock's commanding officer was furious (see source B).

> **B** Quoted and adapted from *The Bloody Game*, edited by P Fussell (1991):
>
> 'Consider yourself under arrest, Lance-Corporal Hiscock. Self-inflicted wound. They'll court-martial you for this. And you'll be lucky if they don't shoot you.' Lieutenant Clarke was, of course, nearly right. I had inflicted a wound on myself, but *I* knew ... that it had been done accidentally. The charge-sheet description of my 'crime', 'Self-inflicted Wound', was one of the most shameful charges possible.

Hiscock was lucky. His story was believed by the court but he was fined ten days' pay.

Waiting to attack

Before an attack soldiers were anxious and afraid. Attacks across open ground against an enemy with strong defences stood little chance of success and the men knew this. Once the attack started, though, many troops have said that their training took over and there was less fear. The waiting, it seems, was the worst part.

> A British soldier wounded at the Somme: 'What I felt was that I had been hit by a tremendous iron hammer ... For a second or two my breath wouldn't come. I thought, this is death.'

> **C** One soldier remembers the night before an attack (quoted in *Death's Men* by D Winter, 1979).
>
> All through that night I never slept a wink of sleep ... I would find myself calculating the chances of survival. Surely a quarter of us would remain unhurt? And the other chances – what are they? Maybe one in three against being killed. One chance in four of being wounded ... and one chance in four of being taken prisoner – as good as escaping scotfree.

The soldier's calculations quoted in source C are very accurate – at least for the British army on the Western Front. French and German casualty rates were rather higher.

The misery of battle

Artillery shells were the weapon soldiers feared the most. They were the biggest cause of casualties. The effect of an exploding shell on a human body was terrible. Artillery shells were designed to explode four or five metres above the ground. Jagged fragments of the red-hot iron shell and the hundreds of shrapnel balls inside them could easily tear off a limb and shatter bones.

High explosive shells could leave no trace of a body at all. This is one reason why the Menin Gate Memorial at Ypres lists the names of 55 000 British and Empire dead who have no grave. The names of a further 73 000 British and Empire soldiers are recorded on the memorial at Thiepval

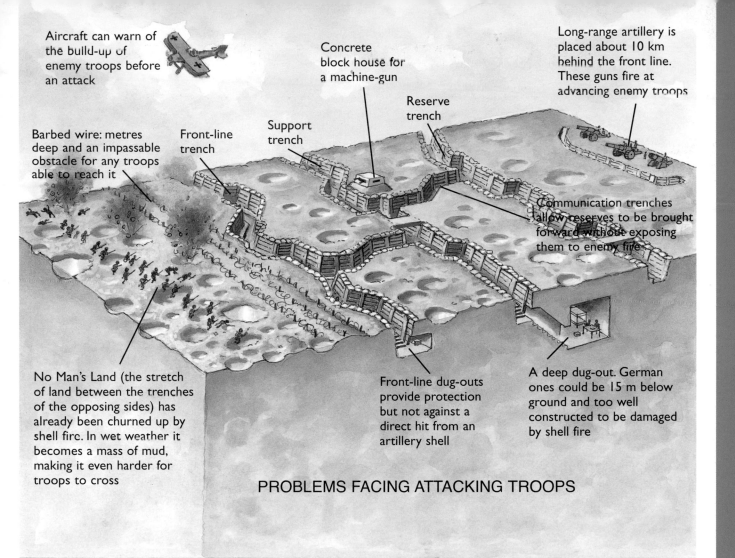

Aircraft can warn of the build-up of enemy troops before an attack

Concrete block house for a machine-gun

Reserve trench

Long-range artillery is placed about 10 km behind the front line. These guns fire at advancing enemy troops

Barbed wire: metres deep and an impassable obstacle for any troops able to reach it

Front-line trench

Support trench

Communication trenches allow reserves to be brought forward without exposing them to enemy fire

No Man's Land (the stretch of land between the trenches of the opposing sides) has already been churned up by shell fire. In wet weather it becomes a mass of mud, making it even harder for troops to cross

Front-line dug-outs provide protection but not against a direct hit from an artillery shell

A deep dug-out. German ones could be 15 m below ground and too well constructed to be damaged by shell fire

PROBLEMS FACING ATTACKING TROOPS

D This illustration shows how difficult it was to launch an attack against a well-defended enemy position and why soldiers feared 'going over the top' so much.

on the Somme. Their bodies were never found – blown to pieces, buried in shell holes and drowned in mud.

It was not unusual for bodies, hastily buried, to be blown up again. Men were buried very close to the lines. If they were lucky, they were later moved to more formal cemeteries in the area. Quite often, though, the record of the burial place – even the grave itself – could be lost. These men, too, would be recorded as among the missing.

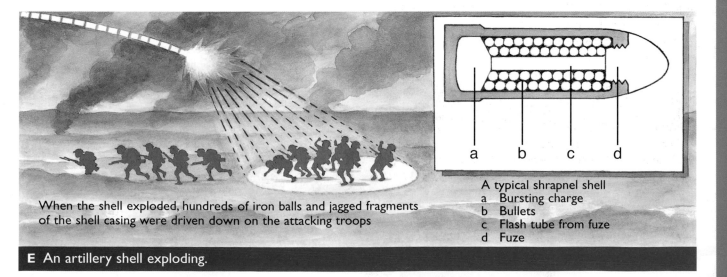

When the shell exploded, hundreds of iron balls and jagged fragments of the shell casing were driven down on the attacking troops

A typical shrapnel shell
a Bursting charge
b Bullets
c Flash tube from fuze
d Fuze

E An artillery shell exploding.

F This photograph is of an actual dug-out recently discovered near Ypres. All the wood is the original from the war. The dug-out was originally German and was part of their defensive line in the Ypres area. It was captured by the British in 1917. Two men slept on each bunk – the four officers, though, had a bunk each. Altogether 36 men and four officers slept in the dug-out which was protected by earth and concrete. It was discovered by accident on the site of a modern brick-works and is in an excellent state of preservation. But the heavy lorries which use the site are gradually destroying the dug-out's foundations.

An experience of Passchendaele

In 1917, heavy rain turned the Third Battle of Ypres (or Passchendaele) into a pointless struggle against nature rather than the Germans. Here was a new hazard for the troops: death by drowning in mud-filled shell craters. (See source G.)

G Captain E C Vaughan recalls his experience of Passchendaele in *Fields of Death* by P Slowe and R Woods (1986).

I paused a moment in the shell-hole; in a few seconds I felt myself sinking, and struggle as I might I was sucked down until I was firmly gripped round the waist and still being dragged in. The leg of a corpse was sticking out of the side, and frantically I grabbed it. It wrenched off and casting it down I pulled in a couple of rifles and yelled for the troops in the gun pit to throw me more.

Vaughan dragged himself out of the shell crater and gathered the few remaining men of his company together. 75 of the 90 men who had begun the attack were either dead or wounded.

After battle

Burial parties were quickly organised after a battle. Corpses could become a cause of disease if they were not buried soon afterwards.

H One man's experience of burying the dead (from *Death's Men* by D Winter, 1979).

As you lifted a body by its arms and legs, they detached themselves from the torso, and this was not the worst thing ... The bodies crawled with maggots ... We stopped every now and then to vomit ... the bodies had the consistency of Camembert cheese. I once fell and put my hand through the belly of a man. It was months before I got the smell out of my hands.

1 This photograph was taken on 1 August, 1917 – the second day of the battle of Passchendaele. It shows British Royal Army Medical Corps stretcher bearers bringing in a wounded man. The battle went on until 10 November. In what ways do you think the mud increased the numbers of casualties?

The wounded

Wounded men – if they were lucky enough to be found before they died – were brought back to the regimental aid post for emergency treatment by stretcher bearers. From there they went to the Advanced Dressing Station. The journey to the Casualty Clearing Station was by ambulance. Here doctors carried out surgery. About half the men who died of their injuries died from head wounds. Stomach wounds were even more deadly with two out of three men dying.

Infection of the wound was a major reason for death from injury. Dirt and fragments of uniform were driven into the flesh by the bullet or piece of shrapnel and often gangrene was the result. Gangrene caused the flesh to rot and amputation – where possible – was one solution. Despite this, 'only' eight per cent of wounded men who received medical treatment died. This was largely due to the courage of the men of the Royal Army Medical Corps. Only three British soldiers have ever won the Victoria Cross twice. Two of these were medical officers.

Q

1 What was a 'blighty'?
2 Why did soldiers despise men who wounded themselves to get out of the fighting?
3 Why do you think Hiscock in source B was still fined, even though the wound was accidental?
4 Can you suggest why mud-filled shell craters during the Battle of Passchendaele were a danger, especially for wounded men?
5 Why do you think the comradeship referred to in source A was such a powerful emotion for men in the war?

How Did Soldiers View Their Enemies?

Stories of German atrocities against the Belgians in the early stages of the war (see Chapter 3) meant that many troops hated their enemy. But in some cases this hatred did not last long. As the war dragged on, soldiers on both sides came to respect each other – they both lived in the same terrible conditions and faced the same dangers. A feeling of 'live and let live' developed in some sections of the Western Front, particularly between the British and the Germans. However, many Frenchmen felt more bitter towards the Germans and it must be remembered that some British troops never lost their hatred for the Germans either.

The Christmas truce, 1914

During the Christmas of 1914 agreed cease-fires took place along two-thirds of the front between the British and the Germans. These were not official truces and were not approved by the High Commands of either side. They simply happened. There were fewer examples of such truces between the French and the Germans.

Though there were further Christmas truces in the other years of the war they were never as many as in 1914. This is because the High Commands tried hard to stop them. The generals realised that it is much harder to kill an enemy once you have exchanged food and cigarettes with him. The British High Command decided to withdraw some of the regiments involved in the 1914 truce from the front line. Sir John French, Commander-in-Chief of the British army until December 1915, was not pleased by news of the Christmas truce of 1914. (See source A.)

During the Christmas truce in 1914 a German urinated on the British barbed wire. He was shot.

B British and German troops meet in No Man's Land on Christmas Day in 1914. The German soldiers shown here are from a part of Germany called Saxony. Saxon regiments had a reputation for being less aggressive than other German regiments – especially Prussian ones. This probably made the truce easier to arrange.

Truces were still arranged, however. Cease-fires to allow each side to collect their dead and wounded from No Man's Land were quite common. Bad weather was another reason for a truce. The struggle to keep trenches from flooding or collapsing was more urgent than the war. Sometimes sides simply agreed not to attack the other in quiet sectors of the front – especially where the trenches were close to each other.

A Sir John French, quoted in *Eye Deep in Hell* by J Ellis (1979):

[I heard of] ... unarmed men running from the German trenches across to ours holding Christmas trees above their heads. These approaches were, in some places, well received by our men and some friendly behaviour took place. When this was reported to me, I issued immediate orders to prevent it happening again.

C One British soldier recalls why a truce had to be suspended (quoted in *The Price of Pity* by M Stephen, 1996).

At about lunchtime, however, a message came down the line to say that the Germans had sent across to say that their General was coming along in the afternoon, so we had better keep down, as they might have to do a little shooting to make things look right!

D A British soldier gives a drink to a wounded German in August 1918. Generally, the wounded were well treated by both sides and given good medical treatment.

There is, on the other hand, plenty of evidence for the hatred that some British soldiers felt towards the Germans. British propaganda had made its mark – although many British troops still respected the fighting qualities of their opponents.

E A soldier recalls a trench fight in *Death's Men* by D Winter (1979). The *Lusitania*, a civilian liner, was sunk by the Germans in 1915. 1200 civilians drowned.

I saw men fighting with spades. The way the Germans yelled was awful. Some made a good fight. Some would crawl on their knees holding a picture of a woman or child in their hands above their heads but everyone was killed. The excitement was gone. We killed in cold blood because it was our duty to kill as much as we could. I thought many a time of the *Lusitania*. I had actually prayed for that day, and, when I got it, I killed just as much as I could.

Q

1 Why was Christmas an obvious time for both sides to have a truce?
2 Apart from Christmas, what other reasons were there for truces?
3 Why do you think the British generals withdrew from the front line those troops who had taken part in the truce in 1914?
4 a) What would have been Sir John French's attitude to the troops in source C?
   b) What would have been Sir John French's attitude to the British troops in source E?
   Explain your answer to both questions.
5 What reasons can you give for the difference in attitude between Sir John French and the men in source C?

The Great War on the Western Front: Outline

This chapter gives an overview of the main military events of the war on the Western Front. Chapter 12 deals with the war on two other fronts: Gallipoli and Italy.

1914

At first the war was what everybody had expected: a war of movement with exciting cavalry and infantry charges. The German advance through Belgium into France was stopped in September, just 60 kilometres from Paris at the Battle of the Marne. This defeat meant that Germany would have to fight on two fronts. It faced Britain and France on the Western Front and Russia on the Eastern Front.

The Germans planned to occupy the Channel ports because these would be useful as U-boat bases. But the British put a stop to the plan at the First Battle of Ypres (October – November). Ypres would be the target of two further battles in 1915 and 1917 but it stayed in British hands. The price, though, was a heavy one since German artillery shelled it into rubble and the town had to be re-built after the war.

Turkey joined the war on the side of the Central Powers (Germany and Austria-Hungary) in November. Both sides now dug trenches from the Belgian coast to the Swiss border (a distance of 700 kilometres). They settled into the kind of warfare that was to last most of the next four years: a war of trenches, barbed wire, dug-outs and machine-guns.

> Australian troops had a reputation for being tough but difficult to discipline.

On the Eastern Front, the Russians mobilised their forces earlier than the Germans expected. This meant they were able to invade East Prussia – German territory. But after a heavy defeat at the Battle of Tannenberg (26–29 August), the Russian advance was halted and then pushed back.

1915

Opinions in the High Commands of both the Allied and Central Powers varied on what to do next. Winston Churchill, in command of the Royal Navy, wanted an attack on Turkey in the eastern Mediterranean to help Russia (see the Gallipoli campaign in Chapter 12). Kitchener, the commander of the army, believed the war could only be won on the Western Front and that the 'Eastern' strategy would be a waste of resources. Churchill led the group known as the 'Easterners' and Kitchener belonged to the 'Westerners'.

At the same time, the German High Command argued over whether to concentrate on the war against Russia or on the Western Front. Generals Hindenburg and Ludendorff argued for an all-out attack against Russia. Their proposal won and General Falkenhayn was ordered to fight a defensive war in the west for the time being.

The battles of 1915 made little impact on the war. A new German weapon, gas, made a surprise and terrifying appearance in the Second Battle of Ypres (April – May). But there was no break-through. The British and the Australian and New Zealand Army Corps (ANZACs) tried to knock Turkey out of the war by landing at Gallipoli in Turkey. It was a complete failure. Italy joined the war on the side of the Allies (the Entente Powers Britain, France and Russia) and opened another front against the Austrians: the Italian Front.

A The Western, Eastern and Italian fronts.

1916

The Germans now reversed their 1915 strategy. They would win the war in the west with a massive offensive. Even if it failed, Falkenhayn told the Kaiser, France would be 'bled white' and forced out of the war. The Allies decided that their best chance of success lay in the British, French, Russians, and Italians all launching big offensives at the same time: June 1916.

1916 saw two of the biggest battles of the war: the German attack on the French at Verdun (February – December) and the mostly British attack along the River Somme (July – November). The Germans failed to capture Verdun and the British and French managed no more than a 13-kilometre advance against the Germans. The Battle of the Somme is noted for the first use by the British of their own secret weapon: the tank.

On the Eastern Front, the Russian General Brusilov had some success with his offensive against the Austrians, causing the Germans to withdraw troops from the Western Front to assist them. In fact, the most important battle of 1916 did not take place on land at all but at sea – the Battle of Jutland (see Chapter 18).

1917

The Allies continued with their 1916 strategy. Indeed, the British Prime Minister, Lloyd George, gave control of the British army in France to a French general, Nivelle. This, he hoped, would make Allied co-ordination more effective. The Germans, on the other hand, went back to their more defensive strategy of 1915. They concentrated on helping the Austrians to try to knock Italy out of the war.

1917 saw further British attempts to break through the German lines with the Third Battle of Ypres or Passchendaele (August – November). However, more important for the outcome of the war were two other events in 1917. The first event was in April when the United States entered the war on the side of the Allies.

The second event was the seizure of power by the Bolsheviks (Communists) in the Russian Revolution. They promised to pull Russia out of the war and agreed a cease-fire with Germany in December. This meant Germany could now concentrate on the Western Front at a time when American troops began to pour into Europe at the rate of 250 000 men a month.

B British troops get some rest in their individual dug-outs.

1918

Ludendorff had realised in 1917 that Germany's only hope of winning the war was on the Western Front. This victory had to come before the United States was fully involved in the war. In the meantime, the British and French generals had run out of ideas and prepared only to defend.

With Russia out of the war, Germany was able to move troops from the Eastern to the Western Front for its massive Spring or Hindenburg Offensive in March. The Allies, including the United States, halted the German advance about 80 kilometres from Paris and then launched their own counter-offensive in August. This involved 430 tanks. The exhausted German army was driven back and Germany's allies began to surrender. Bulgaria surrendered in September, Turkey in October and then Austria-Hungary on 4 November. Finally Germany itself agreed to end the war on 11 November.

Q

1 What was the battle in 1914 that halted the German advance into France?
2 Why was this defeat a serious one for the Germans?
3 How does source A show the difficulties Germany faced in fighting the war?
4 Which event in 1917 do you think was the more important and why: the Russian Revolution or America's entry into the war?

The War on Other Fronts: Gallipoli and Italy

What was the 'weak point strategy'?

In 1915 commanders on both sides realised that any battles on the Western Front would be very bloody affairs with little prospect of success. Instead, they came up with the 'weak point strategy'. Both sides tried very hard to get on their side those countries not yet in the war. Germany persuaded Bulgaria to join it and attack Serbia. Italy joined the Allies and attacked Austria-Hungary. Each side hoped that these new fronts would provide the much needed chance to break through the enemy lines.

Gallipoli

Winston Churchill was in charge of the British navy in 1915. He wanted to attack Turkey through the Dardanelles Straits, seize Constantinople (the

B Anzac Beach, on the Gallipoli peninsula, painted by an Australian war artist. How does this painting show the difficulties the ANZAC forces faced in landing at Gallipoli?

capital of Turkey), knock Turkey out of the war, and so be able to take badly needed supplies to Russia across the Black Sea. It was an ambitious plan but it went wrong from the start.

The Turks had a month's warning of the plan to land troops on the Gallipoli peninsula when an Allied naval attack failed. So when the British and ANZAC (Australian, and New Zealand Army Corps) forces landed on the beaches in April 1915 the Turks were ready for them. They were trapped on the beaches as the Turks fired down on them from the surrounding high ground. 150 000 Allied troops were killed or wounded in the next nine months before the Gallipoli (or Dardanelles) offensive was abandoned.

Churchill resigned as First Lord of the Admiralty. Instead, he served as an officer in the trenches of the Western Front. Gallipoli had proved to be anything but a 'weak point'.

In general, there were no breakthroughs at Gallipoli, the Balkans or the Middle East because these fronts were considered to be side-shows. Neither side

> The Italians and Austrians fought 12 separate battles along the same 60 km wide front in the Isonzo valley.

A The Gallipoli Peninsula. The Allies never got further than five kilometres or so.

C It was not easy to make trenches out of rock. Here the Italians have been forced to build their trenches up rather than dig down. The trench consists of sandbags on a concrete base. An Italian officer is peering through a rifle loophole.

would commit enough men and resources to stage a major offensive in these places. Gallipoli also failed because the Turks got warning of the attack and because the Allied commanders underestimated the toughness of the Turkish troops.

The failure of the weak point strategy was important because it confirmed the traditional thinking of the High Commands of both sides. Each was now convinced that the war would be won or lost on the Western Front. This led to the big battles of 1916: Verdun and the Somme. Unfortunately for the men in the trenches, they went back to same unsuccessful tactics of 1915 – attacks by massed infantry against well defended positions.

The Italian Front

Italy's entry into the war on the side of Britain, France and Russia in May 1915 was a welcome boost. It meant that the Austrians now had a third front to deal with, alongside their Russian and Balkan fronts. There were no dramatic breakthroughs on the Italian front. The Italians and Austrians fought each other high in the mountains that separated Italy from Austria but most fighting took place in the valleys. The Italians launched eleven separate offensives between 1915 and 1917 to cross one river, the Isonzo. Their dilemma was neatly summed up by one historian. He wrote: 'The river could not be crossed until the mountains had been seized, and the mountains could not be seized until the river had been crossed.'

It was the Austrians and Germans who made the breakthrough at the Battle of Caporetto in October 1917. The Italian army collapsed and fell back 130 kilometres before forming a new line, deep in Italian territory. Eventually the Italians were able to reform and counter-attack and severely defeated the Austrians in October 1918, a few weeks before the end of the war.

Q

1 Why were both sides so keen to open new fronts in 1915?
2 Why did the Allied campaign at Gallipoli get off to a bad start?
3 How did the campaign plan to help Russia?
4 Why was the landscape at Gallipoli and on the Italian Front better suited to defence rather than attack?
5 The text gives three reasons for the failure of the Gallipoli campaign:

a) the Turks knew the attack was coming;
b) the Allies did not send enough troops to fight;
c) the Allies underestimated the fighting quality of the Turkish troops.

Explain why each of these three reasons would have helped the plan to fail. Which one do you think was the most important cause of the failure? Explain your answer.

The Eastern Front

This chapter looks at the importance of the Eastern Front for the war as a whole. There is little doubt that if the Germans had just been fighting the British and French (and not the Russians too), the war may have turned out differently.

After some early success against the Germans in August 1914, the Russians were forced back after the Battle of Tannenberg. A second major defeat for the Russians at the Masurian Lakes in September meant that they would have to fight the war on Russian, rather than German soil. The German commanders, Generals Hindenburg and Ludendorff, became national heroes.

Nonetheless, despite these defeats the Russian contribution to the war was already vital. The Germans were forced to withdraw troops from the Western Front to deal with the Russians. This helped the French to defeat the German Schlieffen Plan.

The Russians did better against the Austrians but the Germans quickly came to the aid of their allies. By the end of 1915 the Russian army had retreated 500 kilometres with one million men killed. But the Russians were far from finished. In June 1916 General Brusilov launched a massive, surprise offensive against the Austrians and made some striking advances. Within a week the Russians advanced 60 kilometres and took 70 000 prisoners. Brusilov, though, found it difficult to keep his troops supplied and the Germans and Austrians withdrew troops from other fronts to prop up the Austrian Eastern Front army. The attacks came to a halt in October.

Despite the eventual failure of the campaign, the Russians had again come to the aid of their allies. The British and French were relieved to see German troops withdrawn during the Battles of the Somme and Verdun. The Italians were helped for the same reason. The Austrians lost 740 000 men

▼▼▼▼▼▼▼ Furthest line of Russian advance into Germany

▲▲▲▲▲▲▲ Furthest line of German advance into Russia (line as at January 1918, before the Treaty of Brest-Litovsk)

A The Eastern Front.

B This Russian poster appeals to Russians' sense of history as well as their patriotism. It shows a Russian knight from medieval times slaying the Central Powers' dragon. He has already cut off its Austrian head, cut through the neck of the German and is about to slice off the Turkish head. In the background are the ruins of towns destroyed by the Germans in Europe.

killed, wounded or taken prisoner and it was at this point that the armies of the Austro-Hungarian Empire lost their will to fight. Austria only fought on because the Germans sent troops to help it. However, the Russians could scarcely afford their one million casualties either. The Emperor of Russia, Tsar Nicholas II, was to pay the price for this military failure in 1917 with the loss of his throne and then his life and the lives of his family.

There was a real breakthrough on the Eastern Front in 1917 but it was a German one: Russia's withdrawal from the war. The Tsar was overthrown in March 1917 by a people fed up with the loss of life, and the hardships which the war caused. However, the new government led by Kerensky made the mistake of carrying on with the unpopular war. In November 1917 Lenin and his Bolshevik or Communist Party forced Kerensky from power in a revolution. They agreed a cease-fire with Germany within five weeks. The Germans were now able to move huge numbers of troops over to the Western Front for their final offensive of the war in March 1918.

> Lenin described the Russian troops who deserted in 1917 as 'voting with their feet'.

C These German and Russian soldiers are reacting to the news of Russia's withdrawal from the war in December 1917. The ones with the fur hats are Russians.

The Eastern Front's importance

Russia's role in the war was a vital one, despite its surrender to Germany in March 1918. The Germans had to fight a war on two fronts because of Russia's involvement and this made the threat facing the British and French from the Germans much less serious. Russian attacks in August 1914 and again in 1916 came at crucial moments and forced Germany to weaken its own forces.

D A Russian soldier, Mikhail Rosenthal, describing army morale in 1917 (quoted in *The People's Century* by G Hodgson, 1995):

I didn't feel like fighting any more, there was no one to fight for when Nicholas gave up the throne. It was chaos. The people supposed to give us logistical support [supplies] ran away first. We began to go hungry. We were all very dirty ... At the end of the war there were few people left who could give orders. Our division didn't exist. We were very happy that we were free to run away.

E A Russian general, Alekseev, wrote this report in April 1917 to the Minister of War, after the Tsar had been overthrown (adapted from *Octobrists to Bolsheviks* by M McCauley, 1984):

The situation grows worse every day. Information coming in from all sides indicates that the army is falling apart.

1 Desertions continue all the time ...
2 Discipline declines with each passing day ...
3 The authority of officers and commanders has collapsed and cannot be restored ... the morale of the officers has sunk to a new low.
4 A mood for peace has developed in the ranks.
5 Anti-war propaganda is circulating in the army.

Q

1 Why do you think Ludendorff and Hindenburg were national heroes in Germany?
2 Why were these early Russian attacks helpful to the Allies – even though they were unsuccessful?
3 Compare sources C and D. In what way does source C support source D's view of the Russian army's morale?
4 What makes sources D and E particularly valuable to an historian studying the state of the Russian army in 1917? (Think not just about what the sources tell you but also their provenance. Provenance means the people, place or time the source comes from.)
5 Over what issues concerning the state of the army do both the general and the soldier agree?
6 'The Russian army continued to support the war until the very end.' Using the sources in this chapter and your own knowledge, explain whether you agree with this interpretation.

Key Issue

What was the impact of these new weapons?

The Great War favoured the defenders. Any new weapons mostly helped those who defended trenches rather than those who attacked them. The machine-gun was the supreme defensive weapon.

A brand new weapon like gas made no real impact on the war. It was first used by the Germans in April 1915. It was a total surprise to the Allies and a nasty one at that. But soon they were able to use counter-measures against its effects – though the first of these counter-measures, a cloth soaked in urine held over the face, lacked a certain appeal. The defenders could also light fires along their trenches. The hot air lifted the gas clouds above the men and out of danger. But such methods were not really practical.

Types of gas

The first type of gas used was chlorine. It immediately caused choking and then stripped away the lining of the lungs. Victims died from suffocation. But chlorine had two serious disadvantages: it could be seen and its effect was immediate. By the end of 1915 the Germans had found a more deadly type of gas: phosgene. This was 18 times more deadly than chlorine and could not be seen. Even worse, men who breathed it suffered only minor discomfort at first and therefore breathed in larger doses. Sometimes it was only 24 hours later that the terrible effects took place. The spasms of vomiting could then last for 48 hours. The lungs filled up with yellow liquid and the victims died from drowning.

Gas masks, first introduced in 1916, were effective against both these gases. But no counter-measure was ever found against another German gas, first

A This is an aerial photograph of a typical stretch of the Western Front. The numbers illustrate the following:

1 German front-line trenches.
2 British front-line trenches.
3 A British strong point. This was a heavily defended position to the rear of the lines, ringed by barbed wire and machine-gun positions.
4 Mine craters thrown up by German attempts to explode mines under the British trenches. The craters are surrounded by the chalk typical of the Somme region.
5 No Man's Land.
6 Here the lines were at their closest and this is where the most mines were exploded – by both sides.
7 German forward saps, probably containing listening posts to detect British underground mining operations.
8 British support trenches.

used in 1917: mustard gas. Unlike the others, mustard gas was not that deadly. Only two per cent of its victims died. It attacked the surface of the skin and caused intense burning, swelling of the eyes, blindness and choking. Heavy doses could cause the exposed flesh to be eaten away. From July 1917 to the end of the war, mustard gas caused 14 per cent of all battle casualties.

Nevertheless, the development of the gas mask meant that after 1916 only three per cent of gassed soldiers actually died and 93 per cent were able to return to duty. Changes in wind direction also made it a dangerous and unpredictable weapon since the wind could easily blow the gas back against its users.

The spy in the sky

Aircraft were useful new weapons but they had very little use as *offensive* or attacking weapons weapons. Planes were valuable for reconnaissance or spying missions over enemy lines and occasionally they machine-gunned and bombed troops. They also provided a useful service as 'spotters'. Spotters told the artillery how accurate their fire was and what changes were needed to get the shells to hit their targets. However, it was a slow process because pilots could only communicate with the artillery by dropping messages to them. It could take two hours to spot for just four guns.

Reconnaissance was probably the most valuable role for aircraft. Planes could easily discover enemy troop movements and this could indicate if an offensive was being planned. Aerial photographs were studied for any signs of disturbed earth. Perhaps a tunnel was being dug or new gun pits for artillery were being prepared.

> Fewer than 3000 British troops died in 1918 from the effects of gas.

B The effects of mustard gas are clear from this account by a British nurse (from *I Saw Them Die* by S Millard, 1936):

> Gas cases are terrible. They cannot breathe lying down or sitting up. They just struggle for breath, but nothing can be done. Their lungs are gone – literally burnt out. Some have their eyes and faces entirely eaten away by gas … One boy today, screaming to die, the entire top layer of his skin, burnt from face and body. I gave him an injection of morphine [a pain killer].

C Official statistics for casualties and deaths caused by gas in the British army, 1915–18.

Year	Casualties	Deaths
1915	12 792	307
1916	6 698	1 123
1917	52 452	1 796
1918	113 764	2 673

D The wounded soldier shown in this painting is wearing a smoke helmet, issued in June 1915. It was later replaced by the more efficient box respirator. What sort of problems do you think smoke helmets caused for their wearers?

Q

1 Give two reasons why phosgene was more deadly than chlorine.
2 What important roles did aircraft play in the war?
3 What do you think was the value of aerial reconnaissance photographs like source A to army commanders?
4 Look at source C. Why do you think there are no gas casualties given for 1914?
5 Can you suggest any reason for the sharp increase in casualties in 1917?
6 a) Do these statistics confirm the statement that gas wasn't really a very effective weapon? Explain your answer.
   b) What other statistics would help you to answer 6 a)?

New Weapons: The Tank

The stalemate on the Western Front was eventually broken in 1918 and a new weapon did play a part in this. The new weapon was the tank. To keep it as secret as possible the machine was described as a 'water tank'. Its official title was 'Trench Crossing Machine'. But it was the word 'tank' which stuck. Its major purpose was to break through the enemy barbed wire, clear their trenches with machine-guns and destroy their machine-gun posts. Then the infantry could follow through. Unlike other weapons, this one had a clear role as a weapon of *attack*.

The tank had a maximum speed – on a good road – of about six kilometres per hour. It was protected by about 10 millimetres of steel armour and could carry either four machine-guns or two cannon. Some carried large bundles of wooden stakes, called a fascine, to drop into the enemy trenches so that they could cross them. Others had large hooks which they used to drag away entanglements of barbed wire. Tanks had a crew of eight who had to face many problems. They broke down, got stuck in mud and moved slowly. This made them an easy target for artillery.

The commander of the new tank corps, Lieutenant-Colonel Swinton, wanted to use the tank in large numbers. This, he claimed, would bring the maximum benefit from the element of surprise. General Haig disagreed. He wanted to use them as soon as possible so that the experience gained would help train tank crews in real combat methods. At that time no one really knew what tanks could do and what tactics to use with them.

A The tank had some effect as a weapon of war but it did more as a morale raiser for the public in Britain. Britons flocked to the cinema to see films of these steel monsters which seemed certain to win the war. This one, a Mark Four, is carrying a fascine.

Tanks on the Somme

Haig decided that tanks would be used during the Battle of the Somme in September 1916. The battle was going badly and the tank would be a big boost for the morale of both the soldiers and the civilians.

Only 49 were used in the battle but 17 of these broke down before they even got to the British lines. Of the 32 left, 18 managed to attack the German lines and were successful enough to convince the Allied High Command that they must be used in greater numbers. Haig ordered 1000 tanks to be built. The German High Command was less impressed. At first they made no plans to develop their own but the German troops, it seems, had a different view.

Bullets fired at tanks caused steel spinters to break away on the inside so that the crew had to wear steel masks.

B A German war correspondent (quoted in *The War in the Trenches* by A Lloyd, 1976) wrote:

> When the German troops crept out of their dug-outs in the mist of the morning and stretched their necks to look for the English, their blood chilled. Mysterious monsters were crawling towards them over the craters … Nothing stopped them … Someone in the trenches said, 'The devil is coming', and word was passed along the line. Tongues of flame leapt from the sides of the iron caterpillars … the English infantry came in waves behind.

Tanks played an important role in the final Allied offensive of August 1918 when 430 were used but the losses were very high. There were only six left after just five days but the initial breakthrough had been achieved. The Germans, from now on, would retreat until they surrendered in November.

What did the tank achieve?

Opinions have varied on just how important the tank was as a weapon. Some historians have suggested that it was more successful as a psychological weapon because of the fear it caused among the Germans. Others believe that it was a success because of the way it broke through the enemy lines for the infantry to follow.

C An artist's impression of a British tank attack at the Battle of Cambrai in November 1917. Tanks were used in large numbers in this battle for the first time – nearly 480 of them. Note the role played by British aircraft ahead of the attack.

D Lieutenant F Mitchell was in charge of an improved Mark Four tank during the battle of Passchendaele in August 1917. This is his account of an attack on some German pillboxes – concrete built strongpoints (adapted from *Tank Warfare* by F Mitchell, 1933).

The tank that went for the rear door of that pillbox quickly stuck fast in the mud. As it sank deeper, it fired desperately. By chance, its six-pounder gun turned out to be pointing straight inside the pillbox door at the garrison of 60 men. The walls of the pillbox were shellproof but the door was soon blown away. Most of the garrison was killed by the tank's fire, and few of those who got out escaped the raking machine-gun fire of the sinking tank … There were 29 casualties [among the British troops] instead of a thousand. The tank had shown its qualities.

E A modern historian, J M Winter, had this to say in *The Experience of World War I* (1988) about the effectiveness of the Mark One tanks used during the Battle of the Somme:

The British employed tanks for the first time on 15 September 1916 on the Somme, but with inexperienced crews and impossible ground, they had very little effect.

Q

1 What role was the tank expected to play on the battlefield?
2 What dangers did tank crews face?
3 a) How were the views of Swinton and Haig different on the way the tank should be used?
 b) Which one do you think was right and why?
4 Is source B more in agreement with source D or E? Explain your answer.
5 Sources D and E give different interpretations of the value of the tank. Using sources A–E and your own knowledge, what reasons can you give to explain these different interpretations? (Remember to think about the provenance of the sources. Were they written at the same time? Do they describe the same event? What are the backgrounds of the authors of the sources?)

Extended writing
One historian, Martin Stephen, wrote this about the war: 'The technology of war had … made it very hard to lose a war but even harder to win.' Explain whether you agree or disagree with this view in an essay of about 300 words. You could include the following in your answer:

 a) the effects of the machine-gun, trenches and barbed wire as means of defence;
 b) the impact of gas, aircraft and the tank as weapons of attack.

The Battle of the Somme – Lions Led by Donkeys?

How far was the British attack on the Somme a failure?

A German commander paid tribute to the British troops involved in the Battle of the Somme. He described them as 'lions led by donkeys'. The donkeys were the British generals who planned the offensive. The courage of the British troops was obvious, but was it a fair comment on the generals and especially General Haig – the Commander-in-Chief of the British Army?

The Battle of the Somme was planned by the British and the French together. The French role had to be cut back by about 50 per cent, though, because they were involved in fighting off a fierce German attack at Verdun. Nonetheless, General Haig decided to go ahead with the attack. At the very least, the attack would force the Germans to move troops from their attack on the French at Verdun.

Germany's 'muddy grave'

The first day of the Battle of the Somme, 1 July 1916, was a disaster and it was soon obvious that the offensive would never succeed. 40 000 British troops were wounded and 20 000 killed. Half the troops who attacked on that day became casualties. Most of these casualties happened in the first hour of the attack. Despite this, the offensive went on until November – at the cost of 420 000 British killed and wounded. The French lost 195 000.

Recent historians have taken a more sympathetic view of General Haig and the battle itself. The poor quality of the shells fired by the British artillery during the seven-day barrage – one shell in three failed to explode – was not Haig's fault.

A The map shows that there were some advances before the attacks ground to a halt in November. The question is whether the 13-kilometre advance was worth the 620 000 British and French killed and wounded? What evidence is there in the map that the French attacks did best on the first day of the battle?

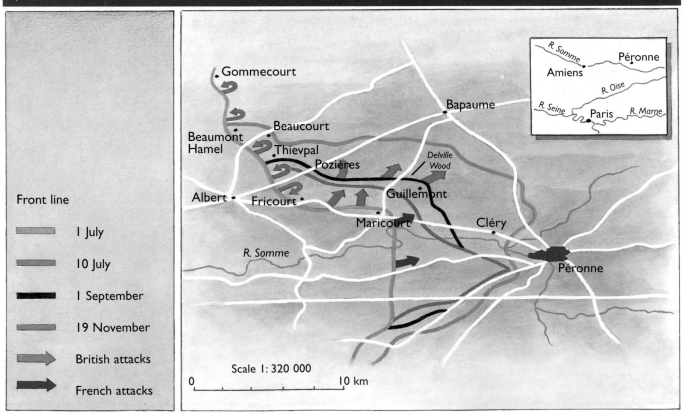

Front line

- 1 July
- 10 July
- 1 September
- 19 November
- British attacks
- French attacks

Gommecourt
Beaucourt
Beaumont Hamel
Thievpal
Pozières
Albert
Fricourt
Maricourt
Delville Wood
Guillemont
Cléry
Bapaume
Péronne

R. Somme

Scale 1: 320 000

0 ———————— 10 km

Inset: R. Somme — Péronne — Amiens — R. Oise — R. Seine — Paris — R. Marne

B A German dug-out captured by the British during the Battle of the Somme. The depth of these dug-outs and the strength of their construction is obvious. The real question is: why did the generals expect such great things from their bombardment when they knew the Germans had defences like these?

The Germans were forced to send troops from Verdun and so pressure on the French was eased.

The German army also suffered heavily, losing many of its best junior officers (captains and lieutenants) among its 650 000 casualties. They could not be replaced. A captain in the German General Staff – the officers who planned the war – commented that: 'The Somme was the muddy grave of the German field army and of its faith in the ability of the German leaders.'

Haig has also been criticised for wasting Britain's secret weapon – the tank – by using them in such few numbers. He should have waited until there were far more available to make a really dramatic impact. But would this have made that much difference? Nearly 500 were used a year later at Cambrai but the attack still failed because the troops couldn't keep up with them. The ground gained was then quickly recaptured by the Germans.

Q

1 What did Haig hope to achieve with his attack?
2 Why could Haig claim the attack was a success?
3 What do you think the German captain meant by the sentence quoted on this page?

Were there alternatives?

The military historian, John Laffin, is one of General Haig's harshest critics. He suggests that Haig should have fought the war more defensively and made the Germans do more of the attacking. In this way Britain would not have lost so many men. Laffin also criticises Haig for his failure to realise the importance of the machine-gun. Haig believed that two machine-guns per battalion (roughly 800 men) was enough. It was Lloyd George, Minister of munitions at the time, who insisted on increasing it to 16 per battalion.

The historian John Laffin described Haig as 'the worst donkey on the British side of the war.'

Another, Paul Fussell, has written that even very simple (and effective) ideas for the Somme attack were ignored. One of these was to stop the British barrage for two minutes before dawn which was when most attacks took place. The Germans, thinking that an attack was about to start, would then begin flocking back to their trenches to set up their machine-guns. Another heavy barrage would then have caught the Germans out in the open.

To rush or not to rush?

The order for the men to attack at walking pace has also been heavily criticised. The French had already developed a technique of rushing in small groups across No Man's Land, dodging in and out of shell holes for cover. This technique, known as 'rushing', limited casualties but needed troops well-trained in these tactics. The British troops who fought on the Somme, Haig believed, were not trained well enough because they were new recruits.

The French did use 'rushing' tactics during the battle – they had a bigger, trained army – and captured the German trenches opposite them in the first hour of the attack.

However, the French success could also be explained by the fact that they had twice as many heavy artillery guns in their sector of the front than the British. The French barrage *was* successful in destroying the German dug-outs. The British barrage, with too few guns, was not. This was the key. Haig, and the man in charge of carrying out the attack, General Rawlinson, believed that the 1.5 million shells fired during the barrage would destroy the German positions. Therefore, 'rushing' tactics would not be needed. There wouldn't be any opposition!

C An extract from *The First Day of the Somme* by M Middlebrook (1971).

After three or four days of continuous shelling, most of the targets should have been destroyed. Of these targets the wire, a vital one for the infantry, was the only one where the damage could be easily assessed ... The reports were inconsistent: in some places the wire was well cut; in others there were a few gaps; but in several places the wire was still intact ... The Germans spotted some of the gaps in the British wire and their machine-guns turned these narrow alleys into death-traps.

D Another historian, N Jones, made the following comments in *The War Walk* (1983):

But all this immense shellfire had not fatally damaged the enemy as the Allied Commanders had fondly hoped; far from it ... Their defences consisted of a vast network of dug-outs, trenches, dormitories dug to depths of forty feet [12 metres] ... This fundamental failure by the British Command to realise the strength of the enemy defences, coupled with the imperfectly cut wire and the rigid parade-ground manner in which the infantry attacked were the main reasons for the horrible failure of the attack.

E In her book *Somme* (1984), Lyn Macdonald writes:

When the mine had gone up and the bombardment had ceased across the whole length of the 8th Corps Front, it was the last signal of confirmation the Germans had needed to warn that the assault was under way. That had happened [the mine exploding under the German lines], not at Zero, but ten minutes before the troops were to go 'over the top'. The Germans had ample time to rush up from shelters and dug-outs, ... ample time to set up machine-guns ... to train guns on the gaps in their own wire and also on the British wire ... through which the Tommies [British troops] would have to pass.

F An extract from *Eye Deep in Hell* by J Ellis (1976).

The British often simplified the Germans' task. To allow the troops to get into No Man's Land it was necessary to cut gaps in the wire just before the attack. As one soldier who was there remarked: 'The advertisement on our front was absurd. Paths were cut and marked ... days before ...' Small wonder the German machine-gun fire was directed with such fatal precision.

G J M Winter's comments, adapted from *The Experience of World War I* (1988):

On the opening day the main problem would be the infantry holding the trenches captured from the Germans, in order to beat off the expected German counter-attacks to get their trenches back. It was for this reason that when the British infantry went over the top early on 1 July 1916 they were weighed down with supplies and were ordered not to run forward.

Why did the British attack on the Somme fail?					
	The British had to cut and tape paths in their own wire before the attack. This tipped off the Germans.	The Germans were able to fire at the gaps cut in the British wire. It was through these gaps that the British had to come.	The British barrage inflicted little damage on the Germans or their trenches.	The barrage did not destroy the German wire to let the British troops through.	The troops were ordered to attack the Germans at walking pace rather than rush.
Source where the evidence comes from.	Found in source F: 'Paths were cut and marked ... days before ...'				

Q

1 What could the British have learned from the French in terms of:

   a) infantry tactics
   b) artillery tactics?

2 Historians make judgements based on the evidence. The five sources above (C–G) provide quite a few reasons why the attack failed.

   a) Your first task is to link the reasons in the top row of the chart above with the sources from which they come.
   b) Which of the reasons given in the chart do you think was the most important in causing the failure of the attack on that day? You should try to answer this by showing how the others were less important. For example, since the German wire was not really destroyed by the barrage, would it have made any difference if the troops had used 'rushing' tactics instead of walking?

3 'The offensive on the Somme was a poorly planned failure because Haig was a bad commander.' Using the sources in this chapter and your own knowledge, explain whether you agree or disagree with this interpretation.

Verdun and Passchendaele

Why were the battles of Verdun and Passchendaele launched?

One of the main aims behind the Somme offensive was to force the Germans to move some of their troops from their attack on the French at Verdun. The Battle of Verdun was an even bloodier and longer battle than the Somme.

Verdun was a city to the east of Paris. The Germans knew the French would defend it to the end. The Germans did not expect to capture Verdun and its 15 surrounding forts. Instead they planned to draw French troops to its defence and then destroy them in such numbers that the French would lose the will to fight. But French morale held on – just.

During the course of the 11-month battle, from February to December 1916, the Germans fired 22 million shells on the forts around the city. The French lost 542 000 men killed and wounded but the Germans lost nearly as many – 440 000. The battle for Verdun represented the strategy of the First World War generals at its most bloody and desperate: to win the war just by killing as many of the enemy as possible.

Two of the French forts took the full force of the German attack in February 1916: Douaumont and Vaux. Source B shows how Fort Douaumont was constructed. It was protected by two layers of concrete 1.2 metres thick with 5.4 metres of earth on top of these. Anyone approaching the fort had to cross a bare slope called a 'glacis' – after getting through 30 metres of barbed wire and across a seven-metre deep moat. It was protected by two heavy guns, set in revolving steel turrets which could also be retracted or lowered, flush with the level of the concrete.

But when the German attack began the fort had been run down by the French and had only a few defenders. It was easily captured in the first four days of the battle and it took the French eight months to get it back. A new commander was appointed, General Pétain. He promised that 'They shall not pass!' and the French stuck doggedly to the task of holding Verdun. The cost, in terms of the morale of the men, came the following year.

A The 75 mm gun turret of Fort Douaumont. Its observation cupola or turret is in the foreground.

B The defences at Fort Douaumont.

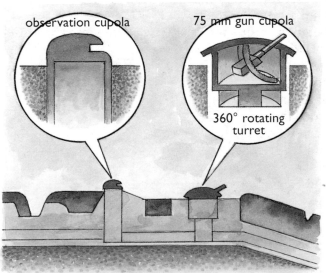

observation cupola

75 mm gun cupola

360° rotating turret

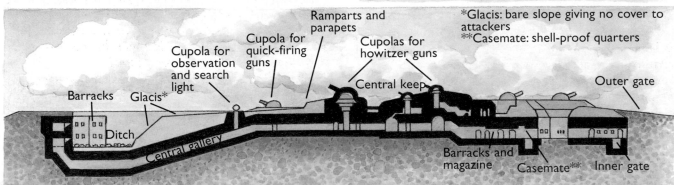

Barracks · Glacis* · Ditch · Central gallery · Cupola for observation and search light · Cupola for quick-firing guns · Ramparts and parapets · Cupolas for howitzer guns · Central keep · Barracks and magazine · Casemate** · Inner gate · Outer gate

*Glacis: bare slope giving no cover to attackers
**Casemate: shell-proof quarters

C A German aerial photograph of Fort Douaumont during the battle. Note what seem to be defensive trenches to the front of the fort.

A lesson of history?

Despite this, the French faith in strong, fixed defensive fortifications was increased. After the war, they built an even more impressive series of forts called the Maginot Line along their frontier with Germany. They were confident the Germans would never get past their Maginot Line, just as they had never captured Verdun. They sat back and let the Germans come at them again – this time in 1940 in the Second World War. But the Germans didn't attack the forts; they simply went round them. The 'fort mentality' belonged to a different war – not the war of rapid tank and troop movements. The French had learned the wrong lesson from the Great War.

> Fort Douaumont had only a skeleton force of 56 men when the Germans captured it in February 1916.

Passchendaele, 1917

In May 1917 mutinies took place in two thirds of the French army. Verdun had taken its toll. A mutiny occurs when troops refuse to obey orders. This was a serious crisis. If the Germans had found out, an attack would have been devastating. Haig decided on an offensive around Ypres to keep the Germans busy in case they found out about France's weakness. The Third Battle of Ypres or Passchendaele, fought from July to November, achieved little more than an eight-kilometre advance and the loss of 300 000 British troops.

Passchendaele is mostly remembered for the appalling conditions. Heavy summer rain turned the battlefield into a sea of mud. Death by drowning in mud-filled shell craters accounted for a great many casualties.

D Edwin Campion Vaughan remembered the suffering of the wounded in *Some Desperate Glory* (1981):

From the darkness on all sides came the groans and wails of wounded men; faint, long sobbing moans of agony, and despairing shrieks. It was too horribly obvious that dozens of men with serious wounds must have crawled for safety into new shell-holes, and now the water was rising about them and, powerless to move, they were slowly drowning.

Q

1 What was the German strategy at Verdun?
2 Why, in theory, was Fort Douaumont so difficult to capture?
3 Look at the photograph of the 75 mm gun turret and its observation cupola in the foreground (source A). How does this photograph show the commanding position of the fort?
4 What do you suppose is meant by the sentence: 'Verdun had taken its toll'?
5 Haig's Passchendaele offensive achieved very little in terms of land gained. Does this mean it was a total failure? (Think about the context of the battle – the general situation on the Western Front.)

Jutland – War Winner?

In May 1916 the only big naval battle of the war took place off the coast of Jutland in the North Sea. Both commanders of the rival fleets were trying to lure the other into a trap with a small number of ships acting as 'bait'. Neither realised that both sides had most of their fleets close by. In this sense, the Battle of Jutland was an accident.

The British Grand Fleet was commanded by Admiral Jellicoe and the German High Seas Fleet by Vice Admiral Scheer. On 31 May 1916 a small force of 40 German ships, commanded by Hipper, met a larger force of 52 British vessels commanded by Admiral Beatty. Each fleet was led by their battle cruisers. These were the most powerful ships after the **Dreadnought** class of super-battleships. The two fleets opened fire at a range of 15 kilometres from each other at about half-past three in the afternoon.

The German gunners were more accurate and, it seems, their shells more destructive. Two of Beatty's battle cruisers, the *Indefatigable* and the *Queen Mary* were sunk by huge internal explosions. A devastated Beatty could only comment: 'There seems to be something wrong with our bloody ships today.'

German shells had pierced the thinly armoured gun turrets of the British ships and started fires. These fires then exploded the ships' magazines – the store deep below decks where the ammunition was kept. The navy commanders in the Admiralty had known about this danger since the start of the

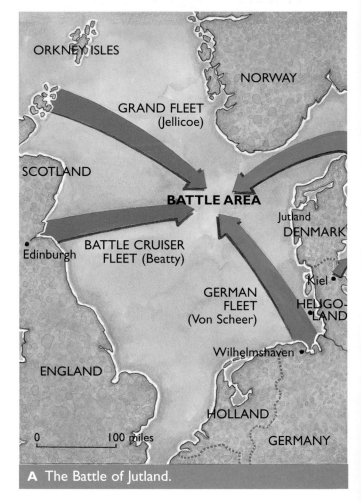

A The Battle of Jutland.

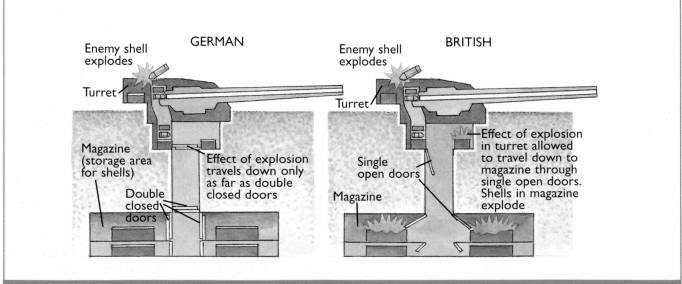

B This illustration shows the differences in the ways British and German gun turrets were designed. What two crucial differences can you see which made the British ships more likely to suffer from exploding ammunition magazines?

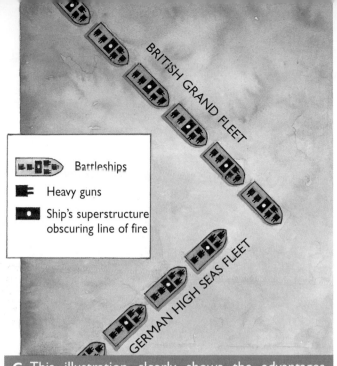

C This illustration clearly shows the advantages which Jellicoe had over the German High Seas Fleet by being able to 'cross the German T'.

war but nothing had been done about it. The Germans found their ships had the same problem but they put it right. *HMS Invincible* was sunk later that day in a similar way. It sank in fifteen seconds, blown in two. All but six of its 1031 men perished with it.

Soon the rest of the two fleets joined in as Scheer and Jellicoe arrived. 250 ships of the Grand Fleet faced 150 of the German High Seas Fleet. Jellicoe had an excellent position since his line of ships came at right angles to Scheer's. This is known in naval terms as 'crossing the T'. Almost all the British Grand Fleet guns could fire at the Germans as they passed at right angles to their ships. The High Seas Fleet gun turrets, on the other hand, couldn't all fire at the British. Those guns at the back of each vessel had their view blocked by the ship's structures and the ships at the back of the line were out of range.

The fight was furious and this time the Germans got the worst of it. Four battle cruisers were quickly put out of action. Scheer knew that his smaller fleet could not afford such losses and he decided to escape from the battle in the early evening mist. Instead, he ran straight into Jellicoe's fleet and both sides lost more ships.

Once again, rather luckily this time, Jellicoe was able to 'cross Scheer's T' and he could have caused yet more damage to the German fleet. But now it was Jellicoe who broke away because he feared a torpedo attack from the German destroyers. Eventually, Scheer managed to get past Jellicoe under cover of night and headed for the safety of port.

Who won?

Jellicoe's losses were much greater than those of Scheer. The British lost 14 ships – three of them powerful battle cruisers – and 6000 men killed. The German losses were 11 ships but only one of these was a battle cruiser. 2550 German sailors died. The Germans claimed a victory because of the heavier British losses. Jellicoe was criticised for letting Scheer get away the second time. Jellicoe, it was said, could have sunk more of the German fleet if he had stayed and fought.

This may be true but would it have mattered? Winning naval battles is about more than tactical issues like sinking enemy ships. More important are the *strategic* consequences which affected the outcome of the entire war. The fact is the Germans were desperate to break the **blockade** of their ports by the British fleet and to set up their own blockade of Britain. After Jutland they could do neither of these. Instead, the British blockade continued without interference from the German fleet, which stayed bottled up in its base at Kiel for the rest of the war.

The German withdrawal gave the Royal Navy control of the seas and it was able to prevent vital supplies reaching German ports. Gradually the German population went hungry and as many as 750 000 German civilians died as a result of diseases caused by their poor diet. This broke the morale of the 'Home Front' and led to food riots in 1918. Morale on the German military front collapsed as a result. The British naval blockade was, therefore, a key factor in Germany's surrender in November 1918. These were the strategic consequences of Jutland.

> The battle cruiser *Lion* only managed to escape destruction because a gun turret officer, despite having lost both legs, ordered the ammunition store to be flooded.

Q

1 Why could the Battle of Jutland be described as an accident?
2 What two fatal design weaknesses did the British ships have?
3 Why was Jellicoe's ability to 'cross Scheer's T' such a major advantage? (Look at source C to help you here.)
4 'Jellicoe threw away a great chance to win a decisive victory at Jutland.' Using your own knowledge and the sources in this chapter, explain whether you agree with this interpretation of the Battle of Jutland.

The U-Boat Campaign and America's Entry into the War

This chapter focuses on Germany's U-boat (submarine) campaign and how it was eventually defeated by a mixture of good British tactics and German error. What were the effects of the U-boat campaign on the outcome of the war?

Submarines were another new weapon and they sank a great deal of British merchant shipping. Merchant ships were essential to Britain because it needed to import so much of its food and supplies. At one stage in 1917 Britain had only two months' supply of wheat and flour. Despite this success, the Germans never sank enough merchant ships to bring Britain to the point of asking for peace terms from Germany.

Unrestricted submarine warfare: the *Lusitania*

At first, German U-boats sank only the ships of Britain and its allies. The ships of neutral countries in British waters were not attacked. But in February 1915 the German government declared that *any* ship around Britain would be attacked – including the ships of countries not at war. This is called unrestricted submarine warfare.

This led to a steady rise in the number of sinkings. Up to February 1915, the U-boats had sunk only 10 British merchant ships. In August alone they sank 42 merchant ships. This campaign, though effective in causing severe shortages in Britain, was controversial. For one thing, civilian liners were included in the list of targets. As a result many women and children were drowned. In May 1915 the British passenger liner, the *Lusitania* was on its way from the United States to Britain. It was sunk with the loss of 1200 lives by a U-boat.

The sinking of the *Lusitania* by a German U-boat caused tremendous outrage in Britain and the United States. The British government knew, of course, that the ship was carrying an illegal cargo of ammunition to Britain. This really made it a fair target for a U-boat. The government made no mention of the ammunition and basically lied to the public.

The sinking of the *Lusitania* was a political disaster for the Germans. It added still more evidence

A A recruitment poster from 1915.

to the British campaign to portray the Germans as barbarians and murderers. It also enraged US opinion because, among the dead, were 128 Americans. The United States was not a country the Germans could afford to anger.

The British government, though, must also share some guilt in the affair because the ship was carrying some ammunition for Britain. This, like the sinking of a civilian ship, was against the rules of war at the time. It also helps to explain why the ship sank in less than 20 minutes.

Anti-submarine measures

The British navy tried desperately to come up with ideas to beat the U-boat threat. Feelings against

MEN OF BRITAIN!
WILL YOU STAND THIS?

Nº 2 Wykeham Street, SCARBOROUGH, after the German bombardment on Dec. 16th. It was the Home of a Working Man. Four People were killed in this House including the Wife, aged 58, and Two Children, the youngest aged 5.

78 Women & Children were killed and 228 Women & Children were wounded by the German Raiders

ENLIST NOW

B The German shelling of English east coast towns like Scarborough in 1914 provided the British government with wonderful material for its propaganda campaign. What feelings is this poster trying to arouse among 'the men of Britain'?

the German navy were running high – and not just because of the activities of the U-boats. In December 1914 German cruisers had shelled three English east coast towns, killing and wounding 700 civilians.

As a defence against U-boats, the depth charge – an explosive device set to go off at a pre-set depth under water – was effective. But they were available only in small numbers and the U-boat had to be located first. That was the hardest task of all. Hydrophones were being developed to detect the sound of U-boat engines under water but they were not yet sensitive enough.

Another anti-submarine measure was the Q-ship, which to begin with proved fairly successful. A Q-ship was a warship disguised as an unarmed merchant ship. U-boat commanders preferred to sink merchant ships by surfacing and using their deck gun. In this way they could save their supply of torpedoes for more dangerous targets such as cruisers or battleships.

When a U-boat surfaced for an easy 'kill' against what it thought was an unarmed merchant ship, the more powerful guns of the Q-ship would blast it out of the water. Equipping ordinary merchant ships with guns of their own also helped to dis-

courage surface attacks. U-boat commanders, therefore, soon learned to be more cautious and had to decide whether a lone merchant ship was really worth a precious torpedo.

> German U-boat commanders sometimes treated the crew of armed merchant ships as terrorists and blasted their lifeboats out of the water.

However, these measures were not really very effective. Only 15 U-boats were sunk in the whole of 1916. By the end of that year Germany had 140 submarines. What really saved Britain was the German worry about the attitude of the United States to German attacks on their ships. The Germans suspended their campaign of unrestricted submarine warfare around British waters in October 1915 after American protests. They resumed it in early 1916 and then called it off again in May of that year. Despite this, on average one in every four merchant ships leaving British ports was being sunk.

The convoy system

In April 1917 the Royal Navy introduced the convoy system of grouping merchant ships together and protecting them with anti-submarine warships called destroyers. This was done at the insistence of David Lloyd George, Prime Minister since December 1916. The convoy system proved very effective in discouraging U-boat attacks. In 1918, only one out of every 25 merchant ships was sunk.

Convoys were so effective not because destroyers sank more U-boats. The main reason was because a convoy of 20 ships wasn't much easier to spot in a vast ocean than a single ship on its own. Therefore, a U-boat's chances of sighting a merchant ship were effectively only one-twentieth of what they had been. When a U-boat did find a convoy it had time to attack one or maybe two merchant ships before destroyers began depth-charging it. The rest of the convoy could then make its escape.

Q

1 What is 'unrestricted submarine warfare'?
2 Why were attacks on merchant ships such a threat to Britain?
3 What do you suppose is meant by this sentence about the sinking of the Lusitania: '… this helps to explain why the ship sank in less than 20 minutes'?
4 Look at sources A and B. Which do you think would have been more effective in whipping up anti-German feeling? Explain your answer.

On 1 February 1917 the German High Command decided to gamble, once again, on re-opening its campaign of unrestricted submarine warfare. The Germans believed that Britain could be brought to its knees in six months as a result of the U-boat blockade of British ports. Neutral countries would stop trading with Britain to avoid having their ships sunk.

The end of American neutrality

The United States had stayed out of the war in 1914 and intended to keep out. Americans saw the war in Europe as just another squabble between greedy European powers trying to expand their empires. The war was also very profitable for American companies. The value of goods traded with Britain and its Allies came to a massive 3.2 billion dollars in 1916 – more than ten times the trade with Germany.

Gradually, the view of the American President, Woodrow Wilson, began to change. The overthrow of Tsar Nicholas in Russia in March 1917 helped to bring this about. The Tsar was an **autocrat**. His removal from power and replacement by a democratic government in Russia meant that Wilson could now claim that the war was a war for democracy against the autocratic powers of Germany and Austria-Hungary.

One further development which helped to persuade Wilson and the American people that they should become involved was the 'Zimmermann telegram' (see source E). Zimmermann was the German Foreign Minister. The British got hold of a copy of the telegram and informed the United States about its content at the end of February. The Kaiser was told by his advisers that the policy of unrestricted submarine warfare would probably

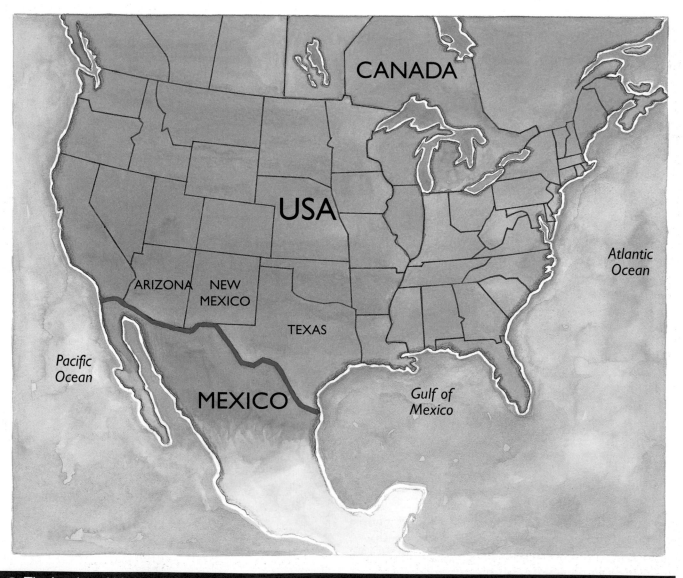

C The border of Mexico and the United States.

bring the United States into the war. They were right. The United States declared war on 6 April 1917. This wouldn't matter, they said, because, by the time the very small American army was big enough and trained, the war would be over. Even if it was not, the United States wouldn't have enough ships left to transport its troops across the Atlantic.

In the short term, though, the situation did not look good for Germany. In 1914, the American navy was the third largest in the world after Britain and Germany. Its destroyers could now be used on convoy duty to protect merchant shipping routes between Britain and the United States. Britain's food supply problems improved immediately. Wheat, for example, could now be imported from the United States instead of Australia, which was much further away. The American government was also willing to lend Britain money so it could buy its vital supplies from the United States – something the Americans had refused to do before 6 April. However, the German advisers got it wrong – eventually. At first, Britain's shipping losses were crippling. 127 ships were sunk by U-boats in March 1917 alone and 211 in August. But Britain's use of the convoy system dramatically cut merchant ship losses and it was not forced to beg for peace. Instead, American troops poured into France in 1918 at the rate 250 000 a month. These fresh and enthusiastic troops were important in the successful Allied offensive of August 1918 which broke Germany's will to fight on.

E Part of the text of the Zimmermann telegram to the German ambassador in Mexico. The ambassador was to pass this on to the Mexican government. The reference to reconquering 'lost territory of New Mexico' is to land lost by Mexico to the United States in a war between the two countries in the 1840s.

Berlin, 19 January 1917

On the first of February we [the German government] intend to begin unrestricted submarine warfare. In spite of this it is our intention to keep the United States neutral.

If this attempt is not successful we propose an alliance on the following basis with Mexico: That we shall make war together and together make peace. We shall give general financial support and it is understood that Mexico is to reconquer the lost territory in New Mexico, Texas, and Arizona.

HELP
STOP
THIS

W.S.S.

BUY W.S.S.
& KEEP HIM OUT of AMERICA
SALESMEN'S WAR SAVINGS DRIVE

D This American poster from 1918 picks on typical propaganda themes: the Germans are shown as murderers of civilians and the destroyers of European culture, represented by the ruins of the church.

Q

1 Look at source C. Why do you think the Germans were so keen to have Mexico declare war on the United States?
2 Why would the states of New Mexico, Arizona and Texas be obvious territories for the Mexicans to acquire?
3 What is the German government asking Mexico to do?
4 How does source E make clear German worries about the American reaction to their intention to re-open unrestricted submarine warfare?
5 What do you think the public reaction in the United States was likely to be to news of the Zimmermann telegram?

Extended writing

'The war at sea played no significant role in defeating Germany.' Do you agree? Write about 300 words on this statement. It will help you to include in your answer the impact of the Battle of Jutland as well as the military and political effects of Germany's U-boat campaign.

Why Did Germany Lose the War?

At the beginning of 1918 no one would have believed that the war would be over within 11 months. It seemed set to go on for at least another two years. But it did end – and with a German defeat. Why? Part of the answer lies with the role of the Americans. There were 325 000 American troops in France in April and two million of them by the end of the war. But more significant was the collapse in morale of the German armed forces and German civilians.

Ludendorff's Spring Offensive

The German High Command launched its massive assault at the point where the British and French sectors joined together. They had the advantage of more men. Ludendorff, the German commander on the Western Front, had been able to bring over 52 **divisions** (about 750 000 troops) fresh from their victory over the Russians. These troops were confident and highly trained in Ludendorff's new 'infiltration tactics'.

The attack, on 21 March, was launched after a very heavy but short five-hour artillery barrage from half-past four in the morning. Ludendorff told his troops not to attack the British lines along the whole 100-kilometre front but to infiltrate in small numbers where the most damage had been done. Where the British positions were still strong, the Germans simply went round them. These 'shock' troops then made for the British artillery and eliminated these so that the rest of the German advance would not be wiped out by the British guns.

The tactics were stunningly successful. On the first day, the Germans broke through the British lines for an eight-kilometre advance – the same distance the British had fought for five months to achieve on the Somme in 1916. The Germans came within 60 kilometres of Paris in late May. But their casualties were as great as the defenders' and the troops soon became exhausted. A worrying development for the Germans was that their hungry troops stopped to loot food from farms. They had moved too fast to be protected by their own artillery. In late July the Allies struck back.

With the signing of the armistice on 11 November 1918, the Germans agreed to give up all the land they occupied on both the Western and Eastern Fronts.

The Allied counter-offensive: 8 August

The British, French, Canadian, Australian and American forces were, for the first time, under the control of a single commander, France's Marshall Foch. This made sure that the Allied troops worked together according to a common plan. The exhausted German troops, faced by fresh Americans and over 600 tanks, gave up. They hadn't had the time to strengthen their defences in the areas they had only just occupied. Germans surrendered in huge numbers. They decided that the war could not be won.

A This photograph shows some Germans taken prisoner towards the end of the war. What does it suggest about Germany's military reserves?

Germany's allies began to drop out of the war: Bulgaria in late September, Turkey in late October and Austria in early November. Kaiser Wilhelm gave up the throne of Germany on 9 November and Germany's new civilian government accepted an armistice at 11 o'clock in the morning of 11 November.

The German Home Front

The German army at the end of 1918 could have fought on, but it didn't want to. The civilian population had turned against the war. The British naval blockade of German ports caused severe food shortages. Many thousands of Germans died as a result of common illnesses because of their very poor diet. Strikes, caused not only by terrible shortages but also by ideas of Communist revolution, crippled industry. The navy mutinied in late October rather than obey a last, desperate order to take on the British navy.

The powerful groups in Germany – the factory owners and landowners – also realised that if they continued fighting a war they could not win, then they risked something worse than a lost war. They risked losing all their wealth in a Communist revolution like the one in Russia in 1917. Hindenburg and Ludendorff shared these worries and they told the Kaiser that the war must end before it was too late.

Germany had launched 'Operation Michael' in March 1918 in the desperate hope that Germany might win the war before the United States could become fully involved. What the Germans had failed to realise was that the United States was already making a real contribution to the Allied cause. It was measured in steel and iron – not troops.

	1916	1917	1918
Britain	200 000	700 000	900 000
Germany	400 000	1 400 000	600 000

B Numbers of workers involved in strikes between 1916 and 1918 in Britain and Germany.

C German women queuing for potato peelings in 1917.

D German civilian deaths as a result of poor diet:

1915	88 000
1916	120 000
1917	260 000
1918	294 000

Allied Powers	Coal (in tons)	Iron (in tons)	Steel (in tons)
Britain	292 000 000	11 000 000	6 500 000
France	40 000 000	5 000 000	3 500 000
United States	455 000 000	30 000 000	32 000 000
Central Powers			
Germany	277 000 000	15 000 000	14 000 000
Austria-Hungary	47 000 000	2 000 000	3 000 000

E A comparison of industrial output by the Central Powers and the Allies in 1914. Note that Russia, who left the war in December 1917, is not included. The figures are in millions of tons.

F A German sailor on the battleship *Helgoland* made these comments in his diary in the second part of 1915 (quoted in *The Great War* by R Tames, 1984):

… the officers have made no sacrifices at all so far … While we have to content ourselves to live on half rations of bread, in the officers' mess [dining room] they hold feasts … at which six or seven courses are served …

All of us wish that the *Helgoland* would run over a mine so that the officers' quarters would be blown to pieces.

Q

1 Why were Ludendorff's 'infiltration tactics' so successful?
2 What does source E suggest about the impact of America's entry into the war?
3 Does source B suggest that strikes were an important factor in causing Germany's defeat?
4 Why was the situation described in source F such a serious one for Germany?
5 'Germany could have avoided defeat in 1918 if it hadn't been for the problems inside Germany itself.' Write a paragraph of 12–15 lines saying whether you agree or disagree with this view.

Women and the Great War: The Home Front

How far did the war really change the lives of women in Britain?

Germaine Greer, a feminist writer of the 1970s, suggested that women in the First World War were a bit like a captive bird whose cage is left open. They had a look outside but decided life was better inside the cage than out.

It is true that women seized the chance offered them by the war to show men (and themselves) what they were capable of doing. It is also true that many of these changes were only temporary and after the war life for women returned to its traditional pattern. What that traditional pattern was depended very much on what class these women came from and whether they were married.

Before 1914

Upper-class women did not work before the war and few worked after it. Working-class women, on the other hand, had to work to help keep their families. They worked before the war mostly in factories and in domestic service as maids. As many as 11 per cent of *all* women worked as domestic servants before the war. The war gave the chance to work in a greater variety of jobs but most of these new jobs were lost at the end of the war.

Fewer married women of all classes worked. In some cases, like teaching, they had to give up their jobs once they got married. But more working-class married women worked than women from other classes. In some parts of the country and in some occupations, such as the Lancashire textile mills, they were expected to carry on working after they married.

Changes after the war

Perhaps the most long-lasting change came about for middle-class women. Before the war middle-class women found job opportunities as teachers, nurses, telephonists, typists, and as sales assistants in up-market department stores. After the war there were better prospects for careers in the higher professions (as lawyers, accountants and doctors) but this change should not be exaggerated. In 1911 women made up six per cent of those employed in the higher professions. By 1951 they had only increased to eight per cent.

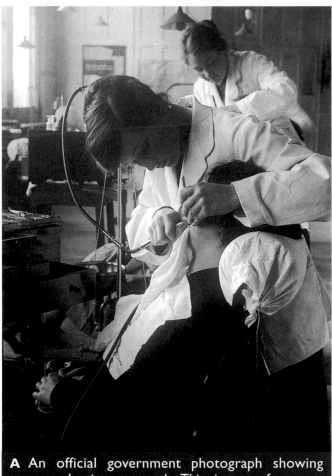

A An official government photograph showing women dentists at work. This image of women involved in exciting new professions is the one often associated with women and the war. The reality for the vast majority was much more ordinary.

In 1919 Oxford University allowed women to study for degrees for the first time. The Sex Disqualification (Removal) Act ended the ban on married women working as doctors, civil servants and solicitors. Women could stand for election to parliament and Lady Astor became the first woman to take her seat in 1919 – though she wasn't the first woman elected. Women over the age of 30 gained the right to vote in 1918 – but men could vote at the age of 21. This difference remained until 1928 when women were able to vote at the same age as men. These improvements, however, meant little to working-class women. They probably welcomed the right to vote but it was the work of courageous pioneers like Marie Stopes who brought real benefits to their lives. In 1921 she

B Women engineering workers. Factory work was not something new for working-class women.

well paid. A female industrial worker could expect to earn between three and five pounds a week – a huge sum compared to the two pounds a *month* for a domestic servant before the war.

> The improvement in women's wages had the disadvantage that fewer women kept their jobs after the war.

C The government encouraged paintings such as this one – titled 'For King and Country' – which shows women munitions workers.

opened Britain's first birth control clinic – but only for married women. Perhaps it could be said that it was only because of the changes in attitude brought about by the war that birth control could be discussed in the open for the first time.

'The Right to Serve'

When war first broke out the government was reluctant to allow women to do any of the jobs left vacant by the men who had gone to fight. Emmeline Pankhurst, a leading **Suffragette**, campaigned vigorously with one of her daughters, Christabel, to have women more involved in the war effort. The Pankhursts organised 'The Right to Serve' procession in 1915 in which 60 000 women took part. The government was soon forced to change its mind and allow women into industry and other traditionally 'male' jobs. It was the only way to keep up production.

The number of women involved in the munitions industry, for example, increased from 200 000 in 1914 to 900 000 by 1918. Munitions work involved the manufacture of shells, weapons, and the handling of chemicals. It was dangerous and unhealthy work. These women were nick-named 'munitionettes' and, more seriously, 'canaries'. This was because the chemicals used turned their skin yellow. But the work, by women's standards, was

D The elder sister of Lilian Miles worked in a munitions factory during the war. She was taken ill and her landlady sent for the doctor (quoted in *The Imperial War Museum Book of the First World War* by M Brown, 1991):

> … he got a specialist to her, and they took her to hospital. She died in terrible agony [of throat cancer]. They said the black powder [in the factory] had burnt the back of her throat away. She was only nineteen.

Q

1 What sort of jobs did women do before the war?
2 Why might married women teachers feel unfairly treated?
3 Why do you think the government was so keen to encourage pictures like the one in source C?
4 a) What do you think would have been the government's reaction to incidents like the one in source D?
   b) Would it have been justified in censoring news of such illnesses among munitions workers?

Women filled all sort of jobs – many of them dangerous. They worked in the shipyards and drove trams, buses and ambulances. 48 000 worked as labourers on the land in the Women's Land Army. These jobs proved women had the stamina and the skill to cope with tasks which people had thought only men could do. Farm work, though, was not a job women flocked to do. 210 000 vacancies remained unfilled.

How much really changed during the war?

Many think that the war created huge numbers of jobs for women in industry and that women took the places of their men who were at the front. But the statistics don't bear this out. Women made up only 31 per cent of the new workers brought in to work in industry. In fact, more women – about 840 000 – found jobs outside industry in commerce and local government, for example. Nonetheless, about 700 000 women did play a vital role in the chemical, metal and munitions industries during the war.

Furthermore, few of these women wartime workers were new to paid work. As many as two-thirds were already in jobs before the war broke out, so the impact of the war on women workers should not be exaggerated. The vast majority of these workers already had jobs.

The skills which women acquired in industry during the war were not that new, either. Few found work in jobs which were really new for women industrial workers. For example, shell-filling in the munitions industry, though dangerous, had already been done by women before the war. Generally speaking, as Jon Lawrence has written, women 'were not acquiring skills which would allow them to compete equally with male craftsmen after the war'.

The post-war 'clear out'

In the first 18 months after the war some 600 000 women left their jobs – most of them voluntarily.

E The official government caption for this Women's Land Army photograph was: 'A gleam of sunshine in the cowshed'. But government propaganda about the delights of farm work convinced only a few. Whatever it was that was gleaming in the cow shed it didn't seem to be sunshine.

F This photograph shows several features associated with the 1920s 'flapper'. She is wearing a short skirt, has a short, masculine haircut, and is smoking.

They accepted that they had been filling in for their menfolk at the front. However, as many as half of the 'new' women workers taken on during the war still had their jobs as late as April 1920. But the economic slump of 1920–21 led to a widespread 'clear-out' of these women workers. In 1921 the percentage of the female population with a job was 31 per cent – one per cent less than in 1911. Only in commercial occupations did women get to keep the jobs they had in the war.

A new generation

Despite this, women did emerge from the war with more confidence in their own abilities. The social and economic changes which women experienced during the war have been exaggerated. But the boost in their self-confidence – at least for middle-class women – could not easily be taken away. In the 1920s a new generation of mainly middle-class young women challenged traditional ideas about feminine behaviour.

These women socialised with men on equal terms, smoked in public and drank in pubs. They went out with men without a chaperone (an elderly female relative, normally) to keep an eye on them. Their behaviour shocked many but these women were determined to stay on the outside of the 'cage' once they had tasted 'freedom'. Their daring allowed other women to make less dramatic but still important progress on the road to equality.

Q

1 What opportunities were opened up for middle-class women after the war?
2 Why do you think women were not very keen on working in the Women's Land Army?
3 What reason does Jon Lawrence give (page 50) to explain why working-class women were unlikely to compete with men for jobs in skilled industries after the war?

22

Women and the Great War: The Military Front

What role did women play in Britain's armed forces?

Nursing

Women were quickly recruited into traditional nursing jobs once the war had broken out. 23 000 women served as nurses close to the fighting and a further 15 000 volunteered to serve as assistants in the Volunteer Aid Detachments. Many upper and middle class women came face to face with a side of life they had never experienced: dealing with the sick and wounded, the dying and the dead.

The work was hard and unpleasant, as one nurse recalled: 'The leg I was holding came off with a jerk and I sat down still clasping the foot. I stuffed the leg into the dressing pail beside the other arms and legs.'

Edith Cavell

Nursing, of course, was nothing new for women. But their closeness to the front did mean that they were exposed to physical danger from enemy action. Edith Cavell is an extreme example of how dangerous this role could be. She was a British nurse who found herself in a part of Belgium occupied by the Germans. She used her role as a nurse to help Allied soldiers stranded behind German lines get back to their own side.

This was obviously not a proper activity for a nurse but the German reaction was very severe. She was tried as a spy and executed in October 1915, despite pleas from neutral countries such as America. Among her final words was the rather puzzling statement that 'patriotism is not enough'. This was another propaganda disaster for the Germans and she became a heroine in Britain. Incidents like this did a great deal to turn opinion in neutral countries – especially the United States – against Germany.

> Two members of the WAAC joined a queue of British troops in France for what they thought was the cinema. An embarrassed soldier had to tell them it was the queue for the brothel.

The women's services

At first the government resisted demands to allow women some role in the armed services as well as nursing and industry. In 1917 it gave in. From the spring of 1917 there were many jobs in the armed services which women were able to do as well. 100 000 women served in the various sections of

A This is possibly the most famous British poster of the war. Published in 1915, it shows women in traditional pose – sadly but proudly urging their men off to war. Women, at this stage of the war, weren't expected to do very much but wave hankies and cry a bit. But Britain's wartime needs soon demanded a more active response from them.

B This British poster of 1917 urged women to join the Women's Land Army. The Women's Land Army involved farm work. It was never popular with British women and posters like this one wouldn't have done much to change their minds.

C This American poster of 1918 is urging women to join the American Red Cross. The image of this open-mouthed, partly undressed, rather sexy nurse is somewhat surprising. It probably wouldn't have been used in Britain.

the armed services: the Women's Army Auxiliary Corps (WAAC), the Women's Royal Naval Service (WRNS) and the Women's Royal Air Force (WRAF). Here they took over the clerical and administrative jobs normally done by men. This allowed more men to go to the front.

Women in the WAAC were thought to be of a lower class than women in the other women's forces. They quickly gained a 'bad' reputation for sexual misconduct with the troops in France. But the 21 reported pregnancies among the 6000 WAAC personnel in France in 1918 suggest that these rumours were somewhat exaggerated. Nothing was said about the men involved in these affairs.

Q

1 Why was nursing an obvious role for women keen to help in the war?
2 Why do you think the execution of Edith Cavell was a propaganda disaster for the Germans?
3 What evidence is there in the text that women were still the victims of double standards about female behaviour?
4 Which of sources B and C do you think would have been more successful in recruiting women to the services? Give reasons for your answer.
5 How might women in 1918 have viewed posters like source A?

Extended writing

'The First World War was a decisive step towards equality for women.' Write 300 words on this view, explaining whether you agree or disagree. You may find it useful to mention the following: women's employment, social and political position in Britain before the war; new job opportunities created by the war; women's social, political and employment position after the war; how much had changed? The information in Chapters 21 and 22 will help you with your answer.

23

The Impact of the War on the Civilian Population

How did the war affect the power of government? How did the war affect living standards?

Before the Great War most politicians had accepted the view that governments should interfere as little as possible in peoples' lives and in the running of the economy. This is one reason why conscription was delayed until 1916. The government believed it should be up to the individual to decide whether he would fight for his country or not. The Great War changed this attitude. The government became involved in a wide range of areas such as industry, food supply and pub opening hours.

Pre-war attitudes

The Liberal Party, led by Herbert Asquith, had been in power since 1905. The Liberals had already begun to change their minds about what the role of the state should be. They believed that the state had some responsibility to help the disadvantaged in society. Asquith's Liberal government introduced measures like pensions for old age (1906), some forms of sickness pay (1912), and unemployment benefit for about 2.5 million workers (1913). The war – as is often the case – led to an even greater change in attitudes towards the role of government.

It is worth pointing out, however, that the government was only really responding to crises as they arose. It did not come up with the new policy first. So, greater state control of industry was something the government had to do because of the munitions shortage. Rationing was introduced because of food shortages.

Lloyd George remained Prime Minister until 1922 but his reputation suffered after the war as few of his promises for a better Britain were kept.

The munitions scandal

The government soon realised that vital industries, such as munitions, railways, mines and shipbuilding, all needed to be brought under **state control**. The public's mind was focused on this issue by the 'munitions scandal' of 1915 when the Commander-in-Chief of the British army, Sir John French, blamed the failure of a British offensive on a shortage of shells.

The immediate political effect of the scandal was that Asquith had to set up a **coalition government** with Conservative and Labour politicians. He was also forced to create a Ministry of Munitions with the Liberal, Lloyd George, in charge.

State control

But the scandal also convinced Asquith that the privately run munitions industry was not delivering enough shells for the war effort. If this was true for munitions, then it was probably true for other industries too. It was accepted that the national interest in ensuring that these were run efficiently was more important than the private interests of their owners. Railways had already been taken over

A This German poster has an unusual theme in its appeal to 'collect combed-out women's hair'. German women were asked to make the sacrifice of cutting their hair so it could be used for insulation and drive belts. At the very least, they were expected to hand over the bits left in their combs.

by the state but many other industries were now controlled indirectly by the government. The government did this by controlling the distribution of certain raw materials, such as sugar, meat, and wool, to factories.

DORA

The government increased its control over people's lives through a series of measures passed through the Defence of the Realm Act (DORA). Through DORA the government was able to take over factories and make them produce munitions. It cut pub opening hours to limit drunkenness. This had been a serious problem because pubs used to open at 5 am and workers could stop off on their way to work. It also ordered beer to be watered down to make it less alcoholic. These measures were effective since convictions for drunkenness dropped to ten per cent of their 1914 numbers. The government also censored the press to make sure that it did not print stories damaging to morale or give away military information to the enemy.

Rationing

The government came round to the idea of rationing reluctantly. It was afraid that rationing food would be very unpopular and that it would support rumours that the German U-boat campaign was bringing Britain to the point of defeat. To begin with, the government encouraged voluntary measures such as growing more food in private gardens or going without meat one day a week. It allowed bakers to save on flour by using flour substitutes instead. These included potatoes. People complained about the taste and the colour of the bread but at least it was never rationed.

In 1917 the government began to respond to the problem of food shortages caused by German U-boat attacks on merchant shipping. The price of a loaf of bread had more than doubled since 1914 and the government ordered a cut of 25 per cent in its price. Controlling prices was certainly new for a British government but the introduction of rationing in 1918 was even more dramatic.

By mid-1918 meat, butter, sugar and margarine were all rationed. This was government control over people's lives on a vast scale – or at least, so it seemed. In fact, the rations laid down were generous and caused little hardship. But the queues disappeared and rationing was popular because people thought it was fairer.

Fines for breaches of the regulations were ferocious. One woman was fined twenty pounds for feeding steak to her dog – and this was at a time when the average male wage was two pounds a week. Getting hold of an illegal extra ration book could lead to three months' imprisonment.

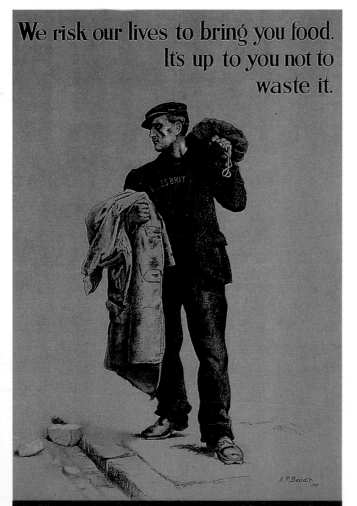

We risk our lives to bring you food. It's up to you not to waste it.

B This low-key British poster reminds citizens of the losses caused by German submarines among merchant seamen bringing food into the country. Note the loaves of bread lying in the gutter.

Q

1 Why was the government reluctant to introduce conscription?
2 What were the immediate effects of the 'munitions scandal'?
3 Why did the government hesitate before introducing rationing?
4 Why was rationing good for morale?
5 In what way did posters like source B help reduce the effects of the German submarine campaign?

What changed?

After the war the nationalised industries (under state control) were returned to their private owners but an important principle had been established: the state had the duty to control some industries for the public good. The Labour government (1945–51) used this argument straight after the Second World War to justify its nationalisation policies. In the short-term, therefore, it seems that not much did change but in the long-term, the change in attitude was significant.

A 'land fit for heroes'?

People also expected a fairer and better Britain after the war. They wanted it to be the 'land fit for heroes' which Lloyd George had promised the returning troops. They wanted better education, better protection against the effects of sickness, unemployment and poor housing. But, on the other hand, people resented government interference in their daily lives, such as the restrictions on drinking, and the high taxes.

The standard tax rate had risen from six pence in every pound to 25 pence by 1918. How could the government bring about a 'land fit for heroes' without the higher taxes and more 'interference'? The government would have found it hard to pay for this new, fair and equal Britain, anyway. Taxes paid for only 11 per cent of the cost of the war. The rest had largely been paid for by borrowing money from the public in the form of government war bonds. The money borrowed would be repaid by the government – with interest – after the war. As a result the government owed, at the end of the war, a staggering 7.4 billion pounds – up from 650 million pounds in 1914. On top of this, the government had the cost of widows' war pensions to pay.

How did the war affect living standards?

On average, wages rose by some 90 per cent during the course of the war but the cost of living rose by 110 per cent. This alone suggests that living standards fell by 20 per cent. However, there were factors which meant that some people's living standards held up quite well. For one thing, rents were controlled during the war and were not allowed to increase above their August 1914 level. This meant that people had more money to spend because their rents stayed the same while their wages increased. This also helped to limit workers' demands for higher wages and reduced

C The problems caused by food shortages are clear from this letter in January 1918 (quoted in *The Imperial War Museum Book of the First World War* by M Brown, 1991):

> A small grocer's shop was 'rushed' a few days ago: I found a huge crowd when I passed – the women and children were packed in a tight mass right out into the road … I asked a woman what was going on. 'Oh, margarine,' said she … It appeared that someone reported that he had margarine, and the whole contents of Newtown slums etc. ran for supplies. He said he had none, and they would not believe him, and one woman slapped his face! At any rate they took all they could before he could call the police up.

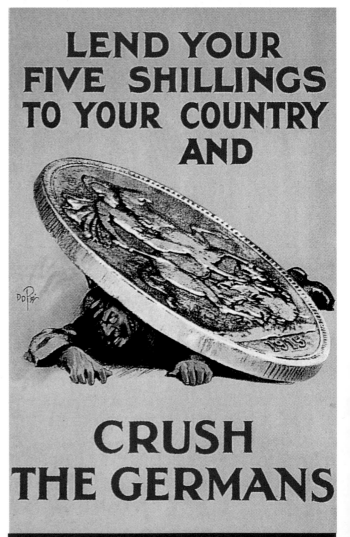

LEND YOUR FIVE SHILLINGS TO YOUR COUNTRY AND CRUSH THE GERMANS

D War bonds: citizens were urged to lend varying sums to the government – in this case five shillings. By investing in this way you made an act of faith in your country's future since, if it lost the war, you didn't get your money back.

Help Them

KEEP YOUR WAR SAVINGS

E This American war loans poster makes the direct link between money lent and bullets for the machine-gun. Americans lent 20.5 billion dollars to their government in such loans.

the number of strikes. Full employment and a lot of overtime also boosted earnings. This is particularly true for women who were now earning far more than they did before the war.

On the other hand, many white collar workers, such as teachers, got no pay increases at all and here living standards fell sharply. The departure of the main breadwinner in the family to the armed forces also caused real hardship where the loss of income could not be made up.

Q

1 Why was the government unlikely to be in a position to bring about the promised 'land fit for heroes' after the war?

2 Compare the two posters in sources D and E. Which do you think would have been more effective in raising money? Explain your answer.

3 a) What does source C suggest about the public's mood in early 1918?

   b) Rationing was introduced to prevent food shortages. What else does this source suggest it might also have been designed to prevent?

Lloyd George and the unions

The government needed to ensure high levels of output in the factories to keep up with the war. To this end, Lloyd George believed that the influence of the trade unions in the workplace had to be reduced. He was particularly concerned with the issue of demarcation. This meant that only skilled workers could do certain jobs in certain industries – even if the job didn't really need much training. These demarcation rules kept skilled workers employed but slowed down production.

The Treasury Agreement, March 1915

Lloyd George arranged a conference with the unions in March 1915 to put an end to these practices. The result of this conference was the Treasury Agreement. Lloyd George insisted on the principle of 'dilution'. This meant that the unions would agree to skilled workers' jobs being done by semi-skilled or even unskilled workers.

Lloyd George was anxious to bring the unions into a sort of partnership rather than bully them. Therefore, the government made concessions too. Lloyd George promised the unions that these changes were only temporary. After the war, the old demarcation system would operate again. He also agreed that the workers doing skilled jobs would be paid the skilled rate even if they weren't skilled workers. This helped convince the skilled workers' unions that the government wasn't doing this to force down wages but only to provide more workers in key jobs.

Lloyd George also banned strikes in firms connected with the making of munitions. By the end of the war there were 6000 such firms. Workers could be fined for going on strike or simply missing work. Skilled workers could not leave for a job elsewhere without the permission of their employer. This was called the 'leaving certificate'. It was the most hated part of a law passed under the Munitions of War Act of July 1915. Any worker who left his or her job without this certificate would have to wait six weeks before starting another

F South Wales miners.

job. Few could afford such a long period without pay. The workers' leaders called this 'slavery'.

The official leaders of the trade unions were willing to make these compromises with Lloyd George. In exchange, Lloyd George promised to tax severely the very high profits made by some employers and to keep down the price of bread. The price of bread, for example, had more than doubled by 1917 from its 1914 price. Lloyd George ordered a 25 per cent reduction in its price. However, some workers believed that the trade union leaders had given away too much. They decided that they would elect their own *unofficial* leaders to represent them. These were known as 'shop stewards'. One trade union, led by its shop stewards, decided to challenge the government.

The carrot …

200 000 South Wales miners went on strike in 1915. Lloyd George declared that the strike was illegal (which it was not) and threatened to arrest the strikers. It was a daft threat, as he soon realised, and he settled the strike by giving in to their demands.

… and the stick

There was also a strike in early 1916 in the shipyards of the river Clyde in Glasgow against the principle of dilution. A meeting between Lloyd George and 3000 shop stewards (unofficial union leaders) achieved nothing – except an accusation from the minister that 'there is German money up there'. Eventually he simply ordered the arrest of the strike leaders and fined any who remained on strike. Lloyd George got away with this because the strikers on the Clyde were all skilled workers and they did not have the support of other workers – unlike the South Wales miners – or the official trade union leaders.

Consequences

The war did a great deal for both trade unions and the Labour Party. Unions before 1914 were not really an accepted part of British society. But the moderate and patriotic role played by the official trade union movement during the war convinced many that the unions were not out to create chaos and revolution. Membership between 1914 and 1919 doubled to eight million.

The Labour Party's reputation increased for much the same reason. Labour ministers in Lloyd George's coalition government showed that socialists could be responsible and patriotic. In 1924 Britain had its first Labour government. The Lloyd George Liberal government which ended in 1922

was the last one in Britain to date (1997). Labour replaced the Liberals as the main opposition to the Conservatives.

Immediately after the war, the mines were returned to their private owners. The miners demanded that the mines stay under state control and that the miners should run them. The war had proved, they claimed, that state control of industries worked for the benefit of all the people and not just their wealthy owners. The miners, though, would have to wait until 1947 for this.

G These statistics refer to the number of days lost in strikes during the First World War. Three million days lost in 1915 could be caused, for example, by one million workers going on strike for three days.	
1914	9 900 000
1915	3 000 000
1916	2 400 000
1917	5 600 000
1918	5 900 000

1 What do you suppose Lloyd George meant by the claim that there was 'German money' behind the strikers on the Clyde?

2 Look at source G.

   a) How do you explain the big difference in the number of days lost in strikes for 1914 and 1915?

   b) What do the other figures suggest about the attitude of the workers as the war continued?

   c) What effect do you think news of the strikes might have had on the morale of the troops at the Front?

Extended writing

Write about 300 words in answer to the following question: 'How far did the First World War change the lives of people in Britain?' Include in your answer:

   a) changes in the way government controlled people's individual lives, such as conscription, rationing, censorship and so on;

   b) changes in the status and role of women;

   c) changes in the way government controlled the economy, for example state control of industries; trade unions.

In your conclusion comment on how important and how long-lasting these changes were.

24

The Great War and the Cinema

There have been well over two dozen major films about the First World War. They have portrayed the war in a variety of ways. Some have used the war to tell love stories, others have been comedies, action films, films about comradeship, and films about the pointless waste of war. Many of the best of them were made in the period between the First and Second World Wars.

There are also documentary films about the war. Some were made during the war itself. The most famous – and controversial – of these was *Battle of the Somme*. It opened in cinemas in Britain in late August of 1916 when the battle itself had been going for less than two months. It was controversial at the time because it showed dead and wounded British soldiers.

Battle of the Somme – fact or fiction?

It also showed footage of a British attack leaving the trenches. Two of the men are killed as they clamber out of the trench and two fall dead among their own barbed wire. The public were shocked by this but most felt it was right that they should see what the war was really like. As many as 20 million Britons saw this film in the first six weeks

Recent evidence, though, indicates that this crucial, most shocking 20-second section of the film was shot in a training trench a few weeks later and was, therefore, faked. Despite this, *Battle of the Somme* is still a remarkable film because of the realistic way it showed the war. However, it made no mention of the huge casualties the British had already suffered or that only a tiny area of German territory had been captured.

A This still from *Battle of the Somme* was not shot during the battle itself but was filmed later at a training camp. The public was not told this – though the absence of packs on the men's backs should have made some people suspicious.

B The director of *Battle of the Somme*, Geoffrey Malins, described in 1920 the reaction of the public to his film:

> The British public realised that it was their duty to see the realistic scenes for themselves. They had been told by the press, they had been told by Parliament … but to no purpose. They must be shown; they must see with their own eyes.

Malins believed that the film would inspire the public to support the war with even more patriotism – and it did. Because of this, he probably felt that he was right to film the faked sequence.

The Great War after the war

It is interesting that films which adopted a clear **pacifist** message and opposed the war were far fewer in number than the other types of film. This may have been because such films didn't make good box office investments. Perhaps people didn't want to go to see films which portrayed the Great War as a tragic waste of life which served no useful purpose. Perhaps it was an event too fresh in people's memories and so too painful to be described in this way.

Films which showed the war in romantic, comic, or heroic terms were more acceptable to the public and therefore to the film-makers. This was a war with the brutal realism and the slaughter taken out. The Great War soon became the Great Myth. Poems and novels about the war tended to adopt a more honest and realistic view of the war but these were not read by millions of people in the same way that films were seen by tens of millions of people. The cinema was a mass entertainment industry.

C Gary Cooper from *Sergeant York*, Warner Bros. This film was based on the war record of a decorated American war hero who captured over 100 Germans on his own.

All Quiet on the Western Front

Perhaps it is not an accident that the best war film of the inter-war years was made from a novel: *All Quiet on the Western Front*. This American film was a faithful adaptation of Erich Maria Remarque's novel, published in 1929. The author was a veteran of the war. It was the one film of the 1920s and 1930s which made no concessions to box office demands for heroism, romance and happy endings. Its message was a pacifist one which portrayed the Great War (and all wars by implication) as an inhumane slaughter.

It tells the story of a group of seven young volunteers who confidently set off, straight from school, for the war. The audience sees the harshness and brutality of their training at the hands of a brutal drill sergeant – the same sergeant who later shows himself to be a coward at the Front. One by one the school friends are killed. The early patriotism and enthusiasm are gradually worn away until the struggle becomes simply to survive. Finally, only the film's central character, Paul, is still alive.

The film ends in October 1918. It shows Paul stretching out from the safety of the trench to reach a butterfly. A sniper shoots him dead. The official High Command's report for the day's events simply records: 'All quiet on the Western Front.'

The film's director, Lewis Milestone, deliberately used unknown actors so that the audience would concentrate on the film's tragic message rather than the actors. An American film which attacked myths about the war, such as heroism and patriotism, might seem particularly bold and risky. But what made the film's anti-war views more acceptable to an American audience was that the film was about German, not American soldiers. It was all right, it seems, for *German* soldiers to become disillusioned and anti-war. Lewis Milestone later went on to make stirringly patriotic films about the Second World War.

The film *All Quiet on the Western Front* caused riots in Germany. Hitler banned it when he came to power.

D This frame from *All Quiet on the Western Front* is one of the most famous final sequences of any film. The hand of the film's central character stretches out to reach a butterfly and then lies still as he is shot by a sniper.

Q

1 Why do you think Battle of the Somme *was such a success in Britain?*
2 *Do you think that Malins' decision to use a faked scene makes his film less valuable as evidence for the historian? Explain your answer.*
3 *What interest do you think a film like* All Quiet on the Western Front *would have for an historian?*
4 *One British historian in 1994 wrote that the film,* Battle of the Somme, *'cheated the viewer' because of the faked sequence. Malins' view in source B is clearly different. What reasons can you give to explain these different interpretations?*

The Hun is at the Gate!
Stand up and take the war

The British poet, Rudyard Kipling, wrote these words when the war broke out. Poems like Kipling's appealed to the average Briton's patriotism and his or her worries about Germany's power. Skilful government propaganda soon turned this worry into hatred. The early months of the war certainly reflected such enthusiastic support for the war. 736 000 men volunteered for the army in the first two months alone.

But Kipling's personal experience of the war quickly changed all this. His only son, John, volunteered for the war – even though, at 17, he was under the legal age of 18. John was killed in September 1915. The news devastated Kipling and his wife. He now criticised bitterly the politicians for not avoiding the war and wrote this poem, 'A Son':

My son was killed while laughing at some jest. I would
  I knew
What it was, and it might serve me in times when jests
  are few.

To some extent Rudyard Kipling's response to the Great War is similar to that of many others. At first, there was tremendous enthusiasm. Then, gradually, people realised that the war would not end soon and that it would be a very bloody one. Although outright opposition to the war was rare in Britain, a sense of bitterness and frustration did develop. The men at the front felt this sooner.

A This epitaph on the gravestone of a Canadian soldier reads: 'Would some thoughtful hand in this distant land please scatter some flowers for me.'

Siegfried Sassoon, one of the greatest British war poets, described the war as 'Hell's Last Horror'.

People today see the war in much the same way. The beautifully maintained war graves in France and Belgium attract thousands of visitors every year. The epitaphs or inscriptions on the tombstones of these men continue to move us and to remind us of just how young they were and how their families missed them.

The gravestones shown are from the Tyne Cot cemetery at Ypres. They are just two of the 12 000 gravestones there. The pain of the families is clear but they express it in different ways.

Britain's dead in *all* wars are remembered every year on the date the First World War ended: 11 November. The poppy – a flower which grows on disturbed, freshly dug soil like that of a grave – has become the symbol of death in all wars but it is the Great War's flower.

The suffering and heroism of the men who died or survived has burned itself into the national memory but this does not mean that it was a war worth fighting. Many historians would agree that the Second World War was a war which had to be fought to rid the world of a terrible evil. It was, in A J P Taylor's words, 'a good war'. Far fewer would say the same about the Great War. Are they right?

In some ways, its memories are bitter ones. The promises made by the politicians for a better life for all after the war never came about. It helped to bring about political movements which later brought terror to Russia, Germany and Italy. It didn't even really bring peace. Twenty years later it was followed by an even more terrible war.

The Impact of the Great War

The war helped to bring about the end of the powerful royal families who had ruled the Austrian, Russian and Turkish Empires. Many people had predicted that these badly run empires were bound to crash anyway but it took a world war to make this happen. The Great War certainly made the collapse happen sooner than it would have done.

Those countries which had bought British goods before the war had found other places to buy these during the war. After the war they either stuck with their new suppliers or began to make the goods themselves. Either way, they didn't buy them from Britain.

The other European powers were affected in similar ways. The war confirmed the United States' position as the world's greatest economic power and speeded up Europe's decline. European governments were faced with huge debts – the Allies had borrowed seven billion dollars during the war from the United States and by 1922 had borrowed another four billion dollars. Promises to build homes and provide jobs for the returning heroes were quietly forgotten by the politicians who made them.

These ex-soldiers became bitter. They felt cheated. Some turned to new political parties such as the communists and fascists because they hated the ruling politicians as much as the soldiers did. After the war, fascists came to power in Italy. There were unsuccessful communist revolts in Germany and Hungary and fascists, led by Hitler, eventually took over in Germany in 1933.

The Treaty of Versailles

An important factor in Hitler's success in Germany was the treaty which ended the war. Germans felt that the Treaty of Versailles, signed in June 1919, was a very severe one. Germany had to accept the blame for starting the war by agreeing to 'the War Guilt clause' (Article 231). Germany then had to hand over all its colonies to the British and French to run. The German army was cut to a token force of 100 000 men. There was to be no German air force, no submarines, or tanks. Ten per cent of Germans and 13 per cent of its territory now belonged to other countries.

The Germans were also told they would have to find over six billion pounds as compensation or 'reparations' for the damage and losses caused to the Allies. German anger at these terms was later used by Hitler to support his attacks on the German government.

B The epitaph on this gravestone reads: 'Sacrificed to the fallacy that war can end war.' A fallacy is a mistake and the relative of this dead soldier obviously drew little comfort from his death in a war which was supposed 'to end all wars'.

Was the Great War a 'good' war?

There were some positive aspects to the war – at least for Britain. The powerful German fleet – seen as such a threat in 1914 – was destroyed by the terms of the Treaty of Versailles. The British people had shown their patriotism and their ability to stick at their duty. They had won a war without losing their commitment to democracy and they had respected the rights of those who opposed the war.

The Germany of 1914 was not as brutal or as nasty a dictatorship as that of Hitler in 1939 but it was still a dictatorship. It still believed in the conquest of other states to increase its own power. General Haig believed that the 'freedom of mankind' was at stake in the war. Perhaps you would expect him to say that but there is an element of truth to it. Would Europe have been a better place if Germany had won the war? If the answer to that is 'no' then the Great War may not have been such a 'bad' war, after all.

All this may be true but whether the Great War was a 'good' one or a 'bad' one is only part of the story. It claimed the lives of eight million men and wounded and damaged the minds of a great many more. Perhaps the last word should come from a soldier who fought in it, for Germany.

The youngest British soldier to be killed was just 14. He lied about his age.

C Erich Maria Remarque, in his introduction to *All Quiet on the Western Front* in 1929, wrote:

This book is to be neither an accusation nor a confession, and least of all an adventure, for death is not an adventure to those who stand face to face with it. It will try simply to tell of a generation of men who, even though they may have escaped its shells, were destroyed by the war.

Q

1 What happened to the ruling royal families of Austria, Russia and Turkey?
2 Why was the Great War bad for the British economy?
3 Why do you think the European governments were not able to provide jobs and homes for their people after the war?
4 What effect did this have on the attitudes of some ex-soldiers?
5 Why do you think the Treaty of Versailles helped Hitler take power in Germany?

Glossary

absolutist – a pacifist who refuses to undertake any activity associated with war (even non-combatant duties)

autocrat – a ruler with absolute or total power

blockade – blocking off a place by surrounding it with troops or ships so that no supplies can get in

censorship – the process of removing information from newspapers, films, books and so on, in order to keep it secret from the public

coalition government – a government formed by two or more parties working together

conscription – a law that requires people to serve in the armed forces

division – an army unit consisting of about 15 000 troops

Dreadnought – the name of a British battleship, launched in 1906. It was so powerful that every other battleship was immediately out of date

mobilisation – getting an army ready to fight

No Man's Land – the land between opposing trenches which neither side controls

pacifist – someone who is opposed to war for moral, religious or political reasons and refuses to fight but may carry out non-combatant duties, such as stretcher bearer

propaganda – persuading people to believe certain ideas and behave in a certain way; sometimes involves telling lies

provenance – where a source comes from. Who wrote it? When? Who was intended to read it? What role did the writer have?

raw materials – materials which occur naturally, such as coal, iron and oil, and which are then used to manufacture something else

reconnaissance – checking an enemy activity, often by using aircraft

socialist – someone who believes that the government should run the country for the benefit of the working people

state control – a policy which involves the government or state taking control of one or more industries

Suffragette – campaigner for the right of women to vote